STUDY GUIDE

for

THE DAILY OFFICE

*

Proposed Book of Common Prayer

*

Clifford W. Atkinson

MOREHOUSE-BARLOW
Wilton, Connecticut

Text of The Daily Office, Rites One and Two (PROPOSED BOOK OF COMMON PRAYER pages 35-107, 115-126, and 136-140) Copyright © 1977 by Charles Mortimer Guilbert as Custodian of the Standard Book of Common Prayer. Reprinted by permission. All rights reserved.

Text of Study Guide Copyright
© 1977 by Morehouse-Barlow Co., Inc.
78 Danbury Road
Wilton, Connecticut 06897

ISBN 0-8192-4076-1

Library of Congress Card No. 77-72493

Printed in the United States of America

Contents

INTRODUCTION 5

    "By the Waters of Babylon"

    "The Love of His True Religion"

THE PATTERN OF THE RITE 7

    To Praise: Invitatory and Psalter

    To Hear: The Christian Year, its Readings and Responses

    To Ask: Prayers and Thanksgivings

BEFORE AND BEHIND 27

SHORTER OFFICES 32

THE DAILY OFFICE 35

Introduction

"By the Waters of Babylon"

At the time of the Exile, the Israelites faced a new and unique problem. They had been removed from their cultic center, but they had been promised, through the prophets, that they would return home. To return, it was necessary to keep the Covenant, and yet the temple was gone. A contemporary Psalmist summed up the problem thus: "How shall we sing the Lord's song upon an alien soil?" (Ps. 137:4).

Up until that time, cultic worship was sacrificial worship. It took place at a temple site where God was known to be. When Naaman returned to Syria, cleansed, and wished to worship the Lord, Naaman took Israelite soil with him to accomplish that purpose (II Kings 5:17ff). This cultic centralization had been emphasized by the reforms of Josiah in 621 BCE (Before the Common Era). These reforms removed local shrines and required that worship be performed only in Jerusalem. Since the prophets had promised an exile of seventy years, it was obviously necessary to develop some way to worship on alien soil. It was out of this necessity that the synagogue rites that underlie the Daily Office came into being.

Whereas the earlier cultic worship required a temple and sacrifice, the pattern that developed by the waters of Babylon needed only a congregation, the scrolls of the Law, and a learned and concerned teacher. The cultic accouterments of priestly caste, altar and sacrificial animals were laid aside until the return. The exiles longed for the return. The Psalmist says: "If I forget you, O Jerusalem, let my right hand forget its skill. Let my tongue cleave to the roof of my mouth if I do not remember you, if I do not set Jerusalem above my highest joy" (Ps. 137:5f). Ezekiel spends the last eight chapters of his prophecy fantasizing about the restored Jerusalem and its worship. Still, the impact of two generations of non-cultic worship left an indelible mark upon the worship of those who derive their liturgical criteria from Holy Scripture.

When Israel returned from exile, the temple was not the first building restored. When they returned, a scribe, a teacher of the Law, took a central place in the restoration. Although the temple was rebuilt, the synagogue remained a central feature in the life of the Israelite nation. The synagogue pattern of Scripture, interpretation, psalmody and prayer sustained Israel, and provided one of the central characteristics of Christian worship.

The pattern of Scripture, interpretation, psalmody and prayer provides not only the basis of that portion of the Eucharist that precedes the Offertory, but the pattern for the Daily Office as well.

Almost as early as we have records of Christian worship, those records tell of the corporate gatherings to perform a service of the Word. Its exact pattern is not always clear, its development is occasionally obscure, it is scarcely universal in application; yet it is unquestionably part of the unbroken tradition of Christian worship.

The watershed development in Western Christian use of the Office is the promulgation of the Rule of St. Benedict as the norm for Western monasticism (around 530 CE). That rule carefully lays out a seven-office pattern, prescribing what was to be contained in each office. That essential pattern, though often "reformed" or "updated", remained constant for about 1000 years in Anglicanism, and remains essentially unchanged in Roman Catholicism to this day.

"The Love of His True Religion"

One of the most significant of the changes wrought by the Anglican reforms and Archbishop Cranmer's work on the Book of Common Prayer of 1549 was the laicizing of the Daily Office. We are told that by the sixteenth century offices were usually grouped, and read publicly, twice in the day. The pattern of the monastic diurnal, however, is fairly complicated, and the services were, of course, read in Latin.

Archbishop Cranmer recreated the Daily Office into a pattern of two complete offices, Daily Morning Prayer and Daily Evening Prayer. He refocused them to include the Reformation concern for Scripture; he restored their commonality by translating them into English. All of this was done, according to the 1549 Preface, " . . . that the people . . . be the more inflamed with the love of his true religion" (PBCP page 866).

It was Cranmer's intent, according to the Preface, that most of the Bible be read in one year. The Psalter was arranged so that it was read through monthly. The rules were kept simple, so that they could be followed easily by everyone, and the form of the rite would not become obscured. All of these purposes are explained in the Preface, which is reprinted on pages 866f of the PBCP. Inasmuch as that Preface can provide a canon, or measuring rod, against which to compare any later developments of the Daily Office, it deserves careful reading by everyone.

The Pattern of the Rite

The pattern of the Daily Office can be looked at in several ways. One is to view it structurally, attempting to determine what comes when, and to ascertain the interconnections of the parts. Another is to view it as a devotional discipline, and attempt thereby to seek out the religious significance of the structure.

To pursue the former first would appear to provide the most appropriate basis upon which to build any other interpretation of the Rite. For this, however, the Rite itself gives some help. The longer introduction to the Confession of Sin in the Morning Office lists the purposes of the Rite: " . . . to set forth his most worthy praise, to hear his holy Word, and to ask, for ourselves and on behalf of others, those things that are necessary for our life and our salvation" (PBCP pages 41, 79. Note that the form in Morning Prayer I includes a phrase indicating the importance of thanksgiving to the Office. Since it is not included in Rite II, it is not included here. This is not to indicate any lack of concern for thanksgiving, but to be sure that what is said of one rite is true also of the other) The whole of the Office, then, is to be described under the rubric of these three verbs: to praise, to hear, and to ask.

Since in the Proposed Book of Common Prayer (PBCP) there are four Offices, it is probably best to note several things. First, the pattern of the four is the same. There are language differences between Rite I and Rite II, but everything remains in the same order. There are no content differences in the Evening Office between Rite I and Rite II. In the Morning Office, the additional material in Rite II consists of a larger selection of Canticles, printed only in Rite II, but available for use in Rite I as well. For all practical purposes, therefore, what is said of one Office is true of all Offices. In the ensuing discussion, the term "Office" should be taken to mean any or all of the Office forms: Morning Prayer I and II, and Evening Prayer I and II.

If one looks with care at the Office, one discovers that there are several ways of beginning and several ways of ending. For the sake of discussion, it is wise to consider these variable beginnings and endings as addenda to the main body of the Office. They affect the tone of the Office. They may indeed change its character, but in the matter of structure and skeleton they are addenda.

The core of the Office begins with the Invitatory and Psalter and ends with the final fixed collect. It is to that core that attention must be drawn. In its simplest outline it appears thus:

A. Invitatory and Psalter
B. Readings, Canticles and Creed
C. The Prayers:
   Suffrages
   Collect of the Day
   Fixed Collects

The three-fold pattern suggested by the Invitation to Confession in Morning Prayer II is obvious in the above outline. First we praise (A), then we hear (B) and finally we ask (C). Insofar as the canticles and creed can be considered interpretation, and insofar as the public recitation of the Office is usually accompanied by a sermon (for which the rubrics provide), the relation of this pattern to that which comes from the waters of Babylon is also clear. It consists of Scripture, interpretation, psalmody, and prayer. From the waters of Babylon until now, this same pattern of praise, Word and prayer is a continuum.

To Praise: Invitatory and Psalter

The Office proper opens with preparatory versicle and response, the *Gloria patri* and (except in Lent) the ancient cry of praise, "alleluia." Taken as the first things said in an Office, the versicles make an exceedingly good opening. In the morning, we request God to "open our lips." In the evening, when the realities of the day's struggles are still with us, we ask God to "make speed to save us." In addition, these versicles point the Office toward God, which is, after all, its appropriate direction. Although Cranmer put great emphasis upon the Office as a source of knowledge of Scripture, the end of that knowledge was the love of God's true religion. It was, for Cranmer, a theocentric, not an anthropocentric knowledge that was to be derived from the study of Scripture implicit in the daily recitation of the Office. That theocentricity is clear when once one considers the Office truly to start with the versicle/response before the Invitatory.

The Invitatory *Venite* originally developed from the use of Psalm 95 as a fixed psalm in the medieval office of Matins. In its entirety, it set a tone of praise and warning. Although it starts as a hymn of praise, the concluding verses are judgmental in character. In the American Prayer Books these verses are dropped, and verses from Psalm 96 substituted. Thus, the whole becomes a hymn of praise opening the Office.

In the PBCP, there are several developments. First, in addition to the *Venite*, the *Jubilate deo*, assigned since 1552 as a reading after the second lesson, and *Pascha nostrum*, derived and expanded from a paschal introit, have been added as alternate Invitatories. Second, *Phos hilaron*, an ancient Greek hymn used in a metric form for over a century in Anglican hymnals, is added to the evening Office as an Invitatory. In that way, the outline of both Offices is the same. The translations in Rite II have, of course, been modernized. The *Venite* of Rite II no longer adds the verses from Psalm 96. Instead, it extends the usual verse choice from Psalm 95 one-half verse, ending that Invitatory "Oh, that today you would hearken to his voice."

The 1928 Prayer Book added a series of antiphons to the *Venite*. These verses had been a feature of the medieval use at Matins, but were dropped by Cranmer. His introduction to the 1549 Prayer Book, noted above, appears to give the explanation. The rite was to be simplified. With the increased seasonal emphasis of both the 1928 and the PBCP rites, the antiphons again have found a place in the Office. The only significant change from the 1928 book to PBCP is the addition of four antiphons. Three are for use during the green seasons (ferial days and the Sundays after Epiphany and Pentecost). The fourth is a lenten antiphon.

The rubric explaining the use of the antiphon uses the phrase, "may be sung or said with the Invitatory." This peculiar use of language is explained by a rubric on page 582, which explains a form of reading the psalter called "Responsorial recitation." In this method, a single voice sings (says) the verses, and the congregation and choir use the antiphon as a response. This apparently was traditionally the way that *Venite* and gradual psalms were sung in the medieval Church. There is a body of music written in this style. It has the advantage, in parishes where choirs perform, of allowing a choir rendition that does not leave the congregation a mere audience. The more usual use of the antiphon, however, is to read it before, and perhaps after, the Invitatory. The rubric on page 141 makes specific reference to using the antiphons as refrains, however, so that one may indeed recapture the ancient use.

Since "metrical versions" of the Invitatories are permitted by the rubric at the bottom of page 141, it is well to list the authorized metrical versions. There is no hymn derived from Psalm 95 in the *Hymnal 1940*. Hymns 278 and 300 are metrical versions of Psalm 100 (the *Jubilate deo*). The former is, according to the *Hymnal Companion* (page 182), " . . . the earliest example in the *Hymnal* of the metrical versions of the Psalms which played such a significant role in the church music of England and America from c. 1560 to nearly 1850." It is dated 1561 in the text of the *Hymnal*. The tune is attributed to Louis Bourgeois in 1551. The latter version, written about 150 years later, has an interesting American history. It was one of the causes of the expulsion of John Wesley from Georgia. He used adaptations of Watts' version of the psalter. The authorities expelled him for "making alterations in the metrical psalms" and "introducing into the Church and Service at the Altar compositions of psalms and hymns not inspected or authorized by any proper judicature" (*Hymnal Companion,* page 195). The text is now properly inspected and is, indeed, authorized as an alternate for use as the Invitatory of the Morning Office.

Phos hilaron comes to us by way of the *Hymnal*. The words themselves are very ancient. It is thought that they may come from the second century CE, although the hymn itself is not quoted until the fourth century, when it is cited by St. Basil (d. 379 CE). He did not know either authorship or date, indicating that it probably was not new in the third quarter of the fourth century. There have been a number of attempts to translate it into English. Two are in the present *Hymnal*. Hymn 173 is the elder of the two, having entered the *Hymnal* in the 1892 edition. Hymn 176 is both more recent in translation, and an addition of the 1940 *Hymnal*. The tune of 176, however, is from the same collection as the traditional Old 100th, which is used for 278 and for the doxology. Both of these may be used at Evensong in place of the *Phos hilaron* as printed.

The *Gloria Patri* is not printed after the Invitatories, and need not be used with them. It would not be used after *Phos hilaron* which is itself a kind of extended trinitarian doxology. The rubrics on page 141 give the ICET and traditional forms of the *Gloria Patri,* both marked for use as two verses. Throughout Rite II the printed text gives the *Gloria Patri* in a one-verse form. The two verse might be preferable in some musical situations.

The Invitatory is the introduction to the Psalter for the day. As was noted above, the Invitatory and Psalter are the prime expressions of praise in the Office. It is for this reason, presumably, that they come early in the pattern of worship. The lectionary provides a balanced psaltery for daily use. If one reads the Office daily, as is presumed by Archbishop Cranmer and all the revisers to the present, the Psalter is read in its entirety within a specified period of time. The present revisers have provided that, "In this lectionary (except in the weeks from 4 Advent to 1 Epiphany, and Palm Sunday to 2 Easter), the Psalms are arranged in a seven-week pattern which recurs throughout the year, except for appropriate variations in Lent and Easter Season" (PBCP page 934). Since the Psalter, like its modern counterpart, the *Hymnal*, is meant to meet many devotional needs, the regular reader of the Office will find devotional help for any and all occasions throughout the course of the seven-week period involved in reciting the Psalter.

Since this is the case, and since we have seen that the Psalter is the prime source of praise in the Office, we had better review an understanding of the meaning of praise. Certainly, for example, Psalm 137, with which we began this study, can scarcely be considered a happy expression. During the course of the Psalter, the Psalmists mourn, moan and lament. They inveigh against their enemies, often in words and phrases that are so bitter that Christians occasionally excise them; yet we say that this is praise.

One thing is clear. Praise is not all alleluias and hosannas. If it were, the Psalter would not be listed as "praise." There is, however, a common thread that runs through the Psalter, regardless of the devotional mood of the individual Psalm. It is a motif of dependency. Regardless of the difficulty that surrounds the individual Psalmist, the solution to the difficulty is always found in trust in and dependence upon God. Psalm 69, for example, which begins, "Save me, O God, for the waters have risen up to my neck. I am sinking in deep mire, and there is no firm ground for my feet . . . " begins its final section, "As for me, I am afflicted and in pain; your help, O God, will lift me up on high. I will praise the Name of God in song; I will proclaim his greatness with thanksgiving. . . . " It may be concluded that, for this Psalmist (and he is not unique), the act of dependence itself becomes the beginning of praise, from which its proclamation comes.

One purpose of regular recitation of the Psalter is to give to the reader of the Office a full awareness of the extent to which God is to be found and praised, even in adversity.

If one is reading the Office only on Sunday, when the Sunday propers are in use, the selection from the Psalter will be shorter, and will, in general, reflect the tone of the rest of the lessons. That selection is, of course, an act of praise, but it is more specifically focused.

As one recites the Psalter, one may either use the *Gloria Patri* at the end of the entire selection, or after each Psalm. In the case of Psalm 119, it is recited after each section if one is using the *Gloria* after individual Psalms.

To Hear: The Christian Year, its Readings and Responses

The lectionary is the core of the Office. It is to this that Archbishop Cranmer particularly directed his attention in patterning and commenting upon the Prayer Book of 1549. The Office, as a service of the Word, builds around the readings.

The lectionary depends in large measure, however, upon the structure of the Christian Year. It is to this latter that our attention must now turn.

THE YEAR

The fullest and simplest description of the Church Year occurs on pages 15-18 of the PBCP. In an abbreviated form it says: "The Church Year consists of two cycles of feasts and holy days; one is dependent upon the movable date of the Sunday of the Resurrection or Easter Day; the other, upon the fixed date of December 25, the Feast of our Lord's Nativity or Christmas Day . . . The Sundays of Advent are always the four Sundays before Christmas Day, whether it occurs on a Sunday or a weekday. The date of Easter . . . determines the beginning of Lent on Ash Wednesday, and the feast of the Ascension on a Thursday, forty days after Easter Day."

In brief, then, there are two festal cycles that include the Sundays of preparation as well as the feast and its associated celebrations. These are separated by Sundays and weeks not associated with festal cycles. Since the typical color for altar hangings, antependia and the like is green, it is simplest to refer to these Sundays and their associated weekdays, simply as the "green seasons." The festal cycles and the green seasons each take up about half of the year.

The Christian Year, then, looks like this:

*Advent, the four Sundays before Christmas

*Christmas, the twelve days from 25 December to 6 January

*Epiphany, the feast and the Sundays following

*Lent and Holy Week, the forty days and six Sundays preceding Easter

*Easter, the feast itself and the "Great Fifty Days" to Pentecost

*The Season after Pentecost, all the Sundays of the year until the beginning of the next Advent

The green seasons consist of the Sundays after Epiphany (excluding the Feast of the Baptism of our Lord, which is always the Sunday after the Epiphany) and the Sundays after Pentecost (excluding Trinity Sunday, which is always the Sunday after Pentecost). Since Christmas and Easter are never the same number of weeks apart in successive years because one is a fixed date and the other can occur anytime between 22 March and 25 April, the number of Sundays separating them varies, as does the number of Sundays from Pentecost to I Advent. The two kinds of seasons differ in that the festal cycles always consist of the same number of days and Sundays, while the green seasons always vary in length. The lessons in the festal cycles, then, can be precisely chosen. Those in the green seasons are subject to shortening or lengthening, depending upon the length of the season. This factor, as well as the inherent differences between a cycle designed around an event and a general reading period, provides the major differences between the kinds of lections one finds in a festal cycle or in a green season.

The Advent Season emphasizes the coming of Christ. In its earlier weeks, this emphasis is upon the Second Coming on the Last Day to judge the living and the dead. This is the traditional thrust of the season, as any reading of the older Advent hymns in the *Hymnal* would indicate. As Christmas comes nearer, there is a shift toward a preparation for the First Coming, in humility, to save the living and the dead. Obviously, the lessons chosen emphasize this seasonal thrust.

Christmas is concerned with the First Coming. The three days following, however, are fixed holy days: St. Stephen, St. John the Evangelist, and the Holy Innocents. These commemorations center around the notion of "witness," since the word martyr means witness. Stephen was the first martyr. Not only is he first in a series that continues to this day, but his was an exemplary martyrdom. He accepted the role, identified it with the suffering and death of Jesus, and thus created the ideal pattern for martyrdom. He was a martyr (as the saying is) by will and deed. St. John, tradition tells us, was the only one of the twelve not to be martyred. John would have accepted the vocation to martyrdom, but was not called. He was a martyr by will, but not by deed. The children killed at the orders of Herod, called the Holy

Innocents, bore witness to the conflict between good and evil that is implicit in the presence of Jesus in a human situation. By their death at the hand of Herod the Innocents showed, in sharp relief, the evil implicit in any sinful human soul. "He who is not with me, scatters," Jesus was to say later. The slaughter of the Innocents is a superb yet horrible example of that truth. The children were martyrs by deed, but not by will.

These three days, along with the Feast of the Holy Name, point toward the Epiphany. The Feast of the Holy Name is celebrated on 1 January. It reminds us that we are saved in the power of that holy name of Jesus and that through his obedience, even to death on the cross, " . . . God raised him to the heights and bestowed on him the name above all names, that at the name of Jesus every knee should bow — in heaven, on earth, and in the depths — and every tongue confess, 'Jesus Christ is Lord', to the glory of God the Father" (Philippians 2:10f). The Feast of the Holy Name witnesses to the power and glory implicit in this humble birth.

The Christmas season ends with the Feast of the Epiphany, which commemorates the arrival of the Magi "from the east." As the celebration of the Nativity began with the angel calling the local shepherds to witness to the wondrous birth, it ends with the star guiding alien astrologers to worship the child Jesus, and to offer their gifts. The local witness of shepherds who praised and glorified God is spread abroad by men from the corners of the world who came to see, and left to witness. This is clearly the traditional understanding of the arrival of the Magi, since in the tradition each Magus represents one of the non-Semitic races known to the medieval world. One is Asiatic, one is African and one is European. Each brings his own gift, and each returns to his world to spread the good news of the birth of a savior.

The Sunday after the Epiphany is a kind of watershed day. It is kept as the Feast of the Baptism of our Lord. As a feast, it looks backward to the previous celebrations. It marks the end of the "pre-ministry" of Jesus. It is also, however, a Sunday after Epiphany, and as such looks forward to the green season to come.

After the Sundays after Epiphany (the last of which always uses the story of the Transfiguration, regardless of how many Sundays after Epiphany there are), Ash Wednesday begins the Easter Cycle. Lent is the season of preparation. Its emphasis is upon discipline, repentance and dedication. It extends for the forty days and six Sundays from Ash Wednesday to Easter. The last week concentrates upon the events surrounding the passion and crucifixion of Jesus. Of all of the seasons of the Church Year, Lent has changed least, in emphasis, content or form, in the simplification of the seasonal arrangement. In Advent, the traditional emphasis upon the Second Coming is heightened. The connection between Christmas and Epiphany as a single sequence receives new impetus in this new arrangement. The Sundays after Epiphany are more clearly a separate season, and absorb the *"-gesima"* Sundays into the general green season. Easter, Ascension and Pentecost are more clearly tied together as the Great Fifty Days. The Sundays after Pentecost receive new coherence by the use of course readings, that is, by reading one Gospel through, more or less in order, during the season. Lent, however, remains much as it always has been: forty weekdays and six Sundays of preparation for the keystone celebration of our faith, The Feast of the Resurrection.

In earlier uses, the Sundays after Easter were very little different from any other series of "Sundays after." Their relationship to the Feast of the Resurrection was tenuous at best. After forty days, the Ascension was kept as a separate event. After ten more days, Pentecost and the outpouring of the Spirit were commemorated. Trinity marked the beginning of months of unrelated Sundays. In the present use, the emphasis is upon the continuity of the Great Fifty Days from Easter to Pentecost. The Ascension is an element of particular importance in the sequence of events that make up that "Week of Weeks" that separate the Christian Passover from the Christian Pentecost. As its earnest of change, there are no longer "Sundays after." There are seven Sundays of Easter, beginning with the feast itself.

Pentecost, like Epiphany, marks the end of the cycle. Like the Epiphany, it is related to, but separate from, the feast which precedes it. Like the Epiphany, it looks forward to the new as well as back to the accomplished. Like the Epiphany, it tends to suffer from comparative neglect when compared to the feast that precedes it. Yet, like the Epiphany, there is a sense in which one may say that the precedent feast cannot be understood or completed without it. Like the Epiphany, the Sunday following is a special commemoration that introduces a green season.

The Feast of the Trinity is a summary of what has been revealed in the witness of Jesus and the outpouring of the Spirit. It also provides the context in which the Sundays after Pentecost may be understood. For, in those weeks after Pentecost, the

Church will read the Scriptures in an orderly fashion and will seek, through the Spirit, to find in them that hope promised by St. Paul to those who would learn their lesson.

THE READINGS

The lectionary selections in festal cycles follow the general thrust of the seasons within the cycle. Those for green seasons are, of course, more general. The rules governing the Daily Office Lectionary are on pages 934f of the PBCP. Along with specific rules for length of lessons and the like, there is a general rubric regarding which lessons are to be used. One major variation in the present structure of the Daily Office is the possibility of reading one three-lesson Office. This is probably the most sweeping change in structure since 1549.

There are, of course, reasons for the change. Ritual changes usually follow changes in customary use. In 1549, for example, it was supposed that the Offices would be read daily and publicly in the parish church building. That certainly remained the custom for a long time. Gradually, however, "recitation" of the Daily Office became, more often than not, a private recitation, in which the Officiant read the Office in the parish office or at home. One can, of course, argue whether or not public worship should have become private devotion, but the reality of an empty edifice prompted the shift. The shift from public worship to private devotion was accompanied, for many clergy at least, by a major change in demands upon their time. The traditional norm of a parish priest in a smallish community acting as the "parson" or "person" in the community shifted to an image of administrator of a congregation, most of whose members, men and women, worked outside the home community. The "parson" became, in many cases, one of the few professionally trained individuals living within the community and able to provide regular leadership for those activities in a community that must, willy-nilly, continue. The demands upon the priest's time were not reduced by the post-World-War-II suburban era; they merely were changed. One reality of the change was the disruption of a regular daily schedule. Of late, moreover, many of the clergy work full- or part-time in a secular job. For them, also, the change in life-style results in a disruption of the pattern of devotional discipline that was learned in seminary. As the move from public worship to private devotion increasingly made the Office a priestly practice, so the shift in clerical responsibilities upset the pattern of devotional life practiced in seminaries and seemed to reduce the use of the Office, even among the clergy.

Both the reduction in use of the Office and the removal of the Office from its basic lay orientation to a clerical one raise significant problems. It certainly was the intention of the 1549 book that the Office be said for the edification of the faithful. Private reading of the Office is merely given as a permissible alternative. More than that, however, the disorganized or occasional use of the Office disrupts that ordered reading of Scripture that was the foundation-stone of the 1549 Office. The aim of any revision ought to be to make the Office more readily available to everyone and to make its use flexible enough that regular participation may be possible for all. After several years of trial use, the single, three-lesson Office appears to have met the need.

For those who wish to use it, the traditional pattern of two Daily Offices with two lessons each is available. For those for whom the single Office provides a more satisfying or successful pattern, it too is available. One thing, however, cannot be stated too often. *The Office is a lay service to be used by lay persons as well as by clergy!!!*

It is important to note that the lectionary provided for the Daily Office is a two-year lectionary. In the course of the two years contemplated for completing the cycle of readings, most of the Old Testament and some of the Apocrypha will be read once. In the same period, the New Testament will have been read through twice. The Psalter is read on a seven-week cycle throughout the green seasons. The lectionary is a three-lesson lectionary. As the PBCP rubric states (page 934), "Three readings are provided for each Sunday and weekday of the two years . . . If two Readings are desired for both Offices, the Old Testament reading for the alternate year is used as the First Reading at Evening Prayer." If one does use a two-Reading, two-Office pattern, the amount of Old Testament Scripture one reads is significantly increased.

The purpose of this lectionary is clearly the same as that of the 1549 book. It provides an orderly reading of Scripture that encompasses the whole of Holy Writ (for all practical purposes) within a defined time. The method of the lectionary, like that of 1549, is to provide course readings. With limited exceptions, each book of the Bible is read in order from beginning to end. The rubric provides that if a holy day intervenes, the lessons that are missed thereby should be made up rather than merely skipped. The only time that course readings are not quite scrupulously observed is on the days immediately preceding and following a major holy day, when the lessons relate to the feast day itself. Each festal season, however, has course readings associated with it for the remainder of the season.

The books chosen for individual seasons in a cycle relate, in general, to the theme of the season. In Lent, for example, one reads either Jeremiah with his constant calls for repentance, or the later chapters of Genesis and the early chapters of Exodus, leading up to the departure from Egypt at the first Passover. One reads either Romans, with its theological interpretation of the death and resurrection of Jesus, or I Corinthians, dealing with the practical implications of living within the Community of the Resurrection while residing in a pagan world. The gospel lessons are those passages of Mark or John which encompass the controversies that made the arrest and crucifixion of Jesus historically inevitable. Similar appropriate choices are made for other seasons. During the green seasons, as has been noted, the scriptures are read in course, book following book, until whatever is not particularly appropriate to a special season has been read. Where there are overlaps in choices, they come in those weeks late in the season after the Epiphany or early in the season after Pentecost that rarely or never occur in the same year because of the date of Easter.

THE CANTICLES

The Canticles are closely associated with the readings and are, indeed, an inseparable response to them. They were an integral part of the medieval Office, and entered the Prayer Book in 1549. There was considerable pressure from the Puritans against the use of hymns not based upon Psalms, so in 1552 the *Jubilate Deo* in Morning Prayer and *Cantate Domino* and *Deus misereatur* in Evening Prayer were added. The first wave of twentieth-century revisions, which occurred between the great wars and which culminated in this country in the Prayer Book of 1928, added considerably to the Canticles. In the 1928 Book the *Benedictus es* was added. Other Anglican books made other additions. Some, in other provinces of the Communion, began to use hymnic material from the Old Testament, especially from Isaiah.

In the 1549 book, there was a rudimentry concern for seasonal Canticles. The *Benedicite* was substituted for the *Te Deum laudamus* in Lent. For the rest, there was only the repetition of the same Canticles daily, with limited variation and no seasonal concern. Even that limited seasonal variation was waived in 1552, when the Lenten restriction on the *Te Deum* was removed.

In the present revision, however, there is a conscious effort both to increase the range of response available in the Canticles and to emphasize seasonal differences. In Rite I of the morning Office, seven Canticles are provided, all in the traditional version. The *Jubilate*, of course, appears now as an Invitatory. The remainder of the Canticles provided in 1928 are there: *Te Deum* (the third section has been omitted, and used later as Suffrages B; this change will be discussed when The Suffrages are under consideration), *Benedicite, Benedictus es,* and *Benedictus.* In addition, the biblical Canticles from the evening Office, *Magnificat* and *Nunc dimittis* are provided, as well as the *Gloria in excelsis.* Any of these may be used, and no differentiation of those to be used after the first or second reading is provided. The rubric on page 47 indicates that, in addition to the above seven, the other Canticles provided in Rite II may be used.

Rite II provides the same seven Canticles that Rite I does, but provides them in a contemporary version. In addition to those, it also provides seven previously unused scriptural hymns in contemporary versions. These are:

The Song of Moses (*Cantemus Domino*) from Exodus 15
The First Song of Isaiah (*Ecce, Deus*) from Isaiah 12
The Second Song of Isaiah (*Quaerite Dominum*) from Isaiah 55
The Third Song of Isaiah (*Surge, illuminare*) from Isaiah 60
A Song of Penitence (*Kyrie Pantokrator*) from Prayer of Manasseh
A Song to the Lamb (*Dignus es*) from Revelation 4
The Song of the Redeemed (*Magna et mirabilia*) from Revelation 15

Of the above, the first has a decidedly Paschal flavor. The First and Third Songs of Isaiah are also used in Advent and Epiphany contexts. The Second Song of Isaiah and A Song of Penitence have a decidedly Lenten flavor. Revelation is, of course, traditionally associated with the Paschal season. Since, of the traditional Canticles, *Te Deum* and *Gloria in excelsis* are not used during Advent and Lent (cf. page 406) and *Benedictus* is among the traditional Advent readings, the seasonal thrust of the fourteen available Canticles becomes clear.

At the evening Office only the *Magnificat* and *Nunc dimittis* are printed. The 1552 additions are eliminated, but the rubrics permit the use of any of the Canticles from the morning Office (pages 65 and 119).

Please note that these Canticles are used after the first *two* readings. If a third reading is used, it is followed immediately either by the sermon or by the Creed. (One assumes that, if the Office is being read privately, the places permitted by the rubric on page 142 for a sermon would be appropriate for meditation.)

In addition to the obvious seasonal thrust, on pages 144f there is a chart of Suggested Canticles which, if followed, provides a balanced use of the available material. Each day of the week has a slightly different tone to it. Friday is, of course, maintained as a day of commemoration of the Crucifixion. In the Suggested Canticles, there are seasonal variations listed as well. The chart provides yet another means of making the daily recitation of the Office a valuable devotional practice for laity as well as clergy.

When the Office is read publicly, the Canticles are often sung. Anglican tradition has covered a spectrum of musical practice in this regard. In many parishes, the Canticles are sung by the entire congregation in one of the *Hymnal* versions. In others, the Canticles have traditionally provided an opportunity for the choir to perform a setting far too difficult for the congregation to join in. If the former provides a closer link to the historical roots of the Office and underlines its essentially congregational and lay character, the latter has, over the centuries, provided moments of particular beauty. The development of Anglican Chant as a particular way of singing Canticles indicates, however, that congregational participation was expected. This is underlined by the fact that Archbishop Cranmer had John Merbecke prepare the *Booke of Common Praier Noted* in 1550. We are told in the *Hymnal Companion* (page 353) that "Archbishop Cranmer desired a musical reform along the line of a great simplification of the traditional melodies so that there should be but one note to a syllable.' " The music from the period indicates that contemporary choirs were able to sing very complex music. Therefore, the only conclusion one can draw is that Archbishop Cranmer was desirous of having the congregations join in the singing. From the beginning, however, there coexisted with these simple melodies settings of beauty and complexity far beyond the musical ability of a congregation.

From the beginning, as well, there were mixed settings, in which a simple tune was sung in one verse, and an exquisite polyphonic version was sung in the next. Thus was preserved both the desire for congregational participation and the creative musical urge. Such a compromise is implicit in the rubrics of the PBCP.

The rubric on page 141 allows antiphons to be used with both the Psalms and the biblical Canticles. The implications of this become clear on page 582 where Responsorial recitation is discussed. There is nothing to preclude a composer from setting the body of a Canticle for choir, with a simple, singable antiphonal refrain. Some music of this sort may, indeed, already be in use. (Psalm 136 indicates that there is some Old Testament tradition for such a custom.)

There soon will be a chant book for the new Canticles and the new versions of the previous Canticles, so that those congregational traditions now in use may be continued.

The Canticles are the response of the faithful to the proclamation of the Word. That proclamation, which is central to the Office has, throughout the history of the Anglican Prayer Books, consisted of orderly reading of Holy Writ for the general edification of the faithful. The clear purpose of this reading is expressed by Archbishop Cranmer: " . . . the people . . . should continually profit more and more in the knowledge of God . . . " (PBCP page 866). Since the whole of Holy Scripture cannot be read in a day, the Creed is recited as the fitting conclusion to the proclamation. The Creed summarizes the biblical faith upon whose proclamation our faith depends.

THE CREED

The Apostles' Creed, which is used in the Office, is the ancient baptismal creed of the Church in Rome. In large measure it is of second century composition. It is a brief expansion of a baptismal formula and probably formed the basis for ancient baptismal instruction. Each phrase can easily be traced to its scriptural source. Unlike the Nicene Creed, it is neither the product of a formal theological conference, nor a universal expression of the universal Church. The Eastern Church has never used the Apostles' Creed. The Nicene Creed was developed by the Ecumenical Councils and agreed to by them specifically to define particular doctrinal points. The Apostles' Creed was, in its origin, much more "occasional," deriving from a liturgical need for an expanded formula at baptism, and a catechetical need for an instructional document.

The Nicene Creed, therefore, in its original form (now restored) begins, "We believe." It does so because the Creed is the universal expression of the universal Church. The congregation joining in that Creed at the Eucharist is proclaiming its communion and community with that universal Church and its universal faith.

In the Office, however, the Apostles' Creed is used, with its "I believe." In that context, the individual hearer of the Word is, in a sense, renewing the vows of his or her baptism, reconfirming the faith by which he or she is saved.

In the Office, as is true throughout PBCP, there are two versions of the Apostles' Creed. Rite I provides the traditional translation. In Rite II, however, the ICET text is used. These versions of the congregational portion of the various services were arrived at by consultation among English speaking Christians from around the world.

A NOTE ON ICET TEXTS

Liturgical change is not confined to the Episcopal Church, or even to the Anglican Communion. All Christian bodies have been reviewing their worship forms. For some, it has been a matter of adopting more formal patterns to supplement or replace their older, freer traditions. For others, it has been a matter of translating traditions and liturgies from other languages (Latin, Greek, Slavonic) into English. From all of this liturgical ferment several substantial interfaith agreements have been reached. For most communions within the Church universal for whom English is the language of worship, those prayer forms used commonly in that worship have been newly translated by the International Consultation on English Texts (ICET). In some communions where formal worship is in its initial stage of introduction, these forms will coexist with older, free church traditions. In some communions where older English forms have been in use, the ICET texts will have to coexist with those older forms. In communions where liturgical forms are firmly imposed, the ICET texts will come into immediate and general use. In PBCP, the pattern of use in the Office is general. The ICET texts are printed for use in Rite II and may be used in Rite I. The traditional forms are printed in Rite I. There are two exceptions to this rule: both forms of the Nicene Creed are printed in Rite I of the Eucharist, and both forms of the Lord's Prayer are printed side by side wherever the ICET text appears.

The development of the ICET texts, along with the development of a common eucharistic lectionary, must rank among the premier ecumenical accomplishments of the latter part of the twentieth century.

When the Creed has been recited, in whatever form, the praise and the proclamation are at an end. The doxological character of the Office has been established by the Invitatory. God has been praised in the Psalms. His Word has been proclaimed in Scripture, in Canticle and in Creed.

As was noted earlier, the framework for the Office is expressed in the Invitation to Confession. There, the elements of the Office are listed as praise, Word and prayer. The first two are provided for by the time that the Creed has been recited. The remainder of the Office is concerned with the Christian work of prayer.

To Ask: Prayers and Thanksgivings

THE LORD'S PRAYER

The section of prayers begins with the salutation and the Lord's Prayer. In the first rite, this is provided only in the traditional form. In Rite II, however, both the traditional form and the ICET version are provided. The Lord's Prayer is always used, except if the Litany or the Eucharist is to follow immediately (as in the rubric on page 142).

In his *Oxford American Prayer Book Commentary*, Massey Shepherd refers to this position for the Lord's Prayer as "the true climax of the service . . . " (pages 16-17). In earlier books, the Lord's Prayer was part of the penitential introduction. In the 1928 prayer book it was used after the Creed where there is no penitential introduction. In some books in the Anglican Communion, the Lord's Prayer is used in both places. The PBCP, however, has settled upon this position as the only one for the Lord's Prayer.

In Saint Luke's Gospel, our Lord teaches the disciples the Lord's Prayer in response to the request, "Lord, teach us to pray . . . " (St. Luke 11:1). Since that time, the Church has considered the Lord's Prayer to be the paradigm of prayers. It is therefore appropriate that it should begin the formal prayer in the Office. There is a sense in which everything that is said thereafter will be an embroidery upon the perfect balance of our Lord's own prayer.

THE SUFFRAGES

Following the recitation of the Lord's Prayer, the Suffrages are said. These are a brief series of responsorial prayers that, taken by themselves, reflect the concerns of the prayers to follow.

In the earlier American Prayer Books, there were two Suffrages in the morning Office, and six in the evening. These were derived from the English Office, which uses the same six, morning and evening. The Suffrages were, generally speaking, adapted from the Psalms. In the PBCP, however, each Office is provided with two sets of Suffrages. The first, or "A" set, is derived from the six evening Suffrages. Several have been adapted to be more inclusive, and one has been added, making the total of seven. These are, of course, derived from the Psalter. The "A" Suffrages are the same at both the morning and the evening Office.

At the morning Office, the "B" Suffrages are derived from the third portion of the *Te Deum*. This section of the hymn has had a peripatetic history. It appeared first as a closing section to the *Gloria in excelsis*. When that hymn was incorporated into the Eucharist, the last section was inappropriate. The words then were attached to the *Te Deum*, where they remained, only slightly less inappropriate. When the decision was made to restore the *Te Deum* to its original form, the problem of the third section remained. It is, after all, a valuable worship text, hallowed by centuries of use. The determination to use it as Suffrages in the Daily Office both preserves the text and finds a particularly appropriate place for it.

At the evening Office an entirely new short litany has been provided. It has a single congregational response. In addition, it adds an element that has been largely missing from Anglican worship since the sixteenth century. That element is the explicit recognition that our prayers are offered in communion with those who have preceded us in service to our Savior, and are now in the Kingdom. It is not an unfamiliar notion, since at the Eucharist we pray " . . . with angels and archangels and all the company of heaven. . . . " The Reformation controversies, however, downplayed the idea. For example, there has been a proper preface for All Saints' Day only since 1928. Now, in the PBCP in general, and in the specific case of the "B" Suffrages at the evening Office, that which is implicit in the common preface of the Eucharist becomes explicit in our worship.

On pages 19-30 of PBCP there is a calendar for the year. In it are listed all of the commemorations of worthies of the Church from the first century to this. It includes all of the biblical saints. It includes the major missionaries to the various parts of the world, and the martyrs who died as a result of their ministry. It encompasses those whose ministries molded the direction of the Church Universal, like St. Augustine and St. Thomas Aquinas, and those whose ministries formed the special witness of the American Church, like John Henry Hobart, James DeKoven and Philips Brooks. In the list are such early worthies as Joseph of Arimathea, in whose tomb Jesus lay, and such recent martyrs as those of New Guinea, who were martyred in 1942. The yearly commemoration of those in the calendar keeps the Church in touch with the reality of its own past. It keeps us tightly connected to our own roots. The list can be used in conjunction with *Lesser Feasts and Fasts*, published by the Church Hymnal Corporation. This volume provides not only appropriate prayers for each commemoration, but a brief biography of each worthy as well. If prayer is to be universal in scope, it must include the whole past of the Church as well as its present and its future.

THE COLLECTS

The earlier Prayer Books provided that ordinarily three Collects were to be said following the Suffrages. One was to be the Collect of the Day. The other two were fixed. This rule was intruded upon in the 1928 Prayer Book which permitted the Collect of the Day to be dropped if the Eucharist was to follow, and required the use of seasonal Collects during Advent and Lent. The phrase describing the material that concludes the Office as coming "after the third Collect" was as much reminiscence as rubrical fact. The PBCP drops the pretence of three and simply provides that "one or more" of the available Collects shall be used. This permits the Officiant to abide strictly by the customary three, or to ignore the tradition completely, and with rubrical impunity.

The PBCP, however, also provides some greater variety of choices.

The Sunday Collects, which are to be used throughout the succeeding week, as well as the Collects for major holy days and special occasions, are found on the PBCP between pages 159 and 261. There are two complete sets, one in traditional language for use with Rite I and one in contemporary language for use with Rite II. The Collect always is for the same week, day or feast as the lessons which have been read.

Instead of two inflexible choices to follow the Collect for the day, the PBCP offers seven alternatives from which to choose. Three are for days of the week: Friday, Saturday and Sunday. Their presence reminds us that every week is a remembrance of the death, burial and resurrection of Jesus our Savior. The Collects remind us of that remembrance. The proposed Canticles underline it. For those who keep them, the Friday fast and Sunday feast reinforce it. The three days are a constant reminder of Saint Paul's teaching that: " . . . when we were baptized into union with Christ Jesus we were baptized into his death; by baptism we were buried with him and lay dead, in order that, as Christ was raised from the dead in the splendor of the Father, so also we might set our feet upon the new path of life" (Romans 6:3-4 NEB).

Of the remaining four Collects, two are the traditional ones associated with the Office since the Middle Ages, and in this position since 1549. In the morning Office, the traditional ones are bracketed by two new Collects, one for renewal and one for guidance. In the evening Office, the traditional Collects precede the two new selections for protection and the presence of Christ. Of these newly added Collects, about half are from the 1928 Prayer Book, where they were placed in different contexts and often not used. The Collects for Sunday and renewal in the morning Office come from the Family Prayer section of the 1928 book, as does the Collect for protection in the evening Office. The Collect for Friday at the evening Office comes from the Burial of the Dead, while its morning counterpart is the Collect for the Monday in Holy Week. Whatever the provenance of the rest, they are not from the 1928 book.

As in the selection of Canticles, the purpose of so broad a selection is to increase the devotional opportunities of those who read the Office regularly. As with the Canticles, appropriate use of the Collects can provide a pattern to the week and a kind of support system to devotion.

The Office in the PBCP, like its predecessor of 1549, requires no specific devotions after the Collects. It is unlike the Office of 1549, however, in that a great deal of optional material is provided from which the Officiant may choose.

This study has, so far, dealt only with the material which is a necessary part of the Office. Taken as an entity, from Invitatory to Collects, the Office stands alone. It can, however, be the vehicle by which a great deal more devotional material may be brought into a life of ascetic discipline. It is to these additional materials, therefore, that attention must now be directed.

Before and Behind

The additional devotional material for the Office is either prepended to the Invitatory or placed after the Collects. The Office may begin in several ways. It may end with a wide variety of prayer forms.

The Office has begun, since 1552, with sentences of Scripture. In the English books, all of the sentences are penitential in nature, since they must lead into the general confession. In all of the American books, however, there have been general sentences. In 1892 the seasonal sentences were introduced. The PBCP carried the American custom to its logical conclusion, by providing enough seasonal sentences to give variety through the longer special seasons and, in seasons with a variety of emphases, to provide for intraseasonal variation. The general sentences, for use during green seasons, provide considerable variety as well.

In the PBCP, however, these sentences become optional, permitting the Office to open with the Invitatory. The reasons for beginning there were noted above. The reasons for beginning with appropriate verses of Scripture, especially during special seasons, are self-evident.

In 1552, Archbishop Cranmer added the Penitential Introduction to the Office. As has been noted, it followed, twice daily, upon a penitential sentence from Scripture. Until 1892, the long exhortation to confession was read everywhere twice daily. In 1892, however, the short exhortation was added to the evening Office as an alternative. The shorter form was added to the morning Office in 1928. In the PBCP there are always two alternatives. At the morning Office there is the shorter adaptation of the 1552 exhortation and the single sentence. At the evening Office, a short exhortation and the single sentence are both available.

One of the major differences between Rite I and Rite II becomes evident when the confession is recited. Rite I uses a very slightly amended 1552 confession. Rite II uses the confession prepared for the PBCP, used in Rite II throughout and often as an alternative in Rite I. For those who followed the progress of revision through the various trial rites, the final form will be seen to be a product of that almost decade-long process.

One of the mixed blessings of formal, liturgical worship is the existence of the fossils of past theological battles, long dead. The long declaration of absolution that used to follow the confession in the Offices is such a fossil. The Puritans denied and decried priestly absolution. The Anglicans affirmed and applauded priestly absolution. In 1604, as part of an attempt to retain both views within the one Anglican Church, the Anglican compromise that assures one that absolution is conferred, without conferring it, was written and included in the Prayer Book. The American Church has always provided alternatives. In the PBCP the 1604 form, slightly adapted, is found in the special liturgy for Ash Wednesday (page 269). It is treated, as it has been since 1662, as a priestly absolution. An alternate form is provided for a lay reader or a deacon who may be officiating. So far as the Office is concerned, however, a simple priestly absolution is provided for each Office. An alternative to be used by deacon or lay person is provided, should no priest be present.

In sum, then, the Office may open in one of three ways. It may open with an opening sentence, the Penitential Introduction and the Invitatory. It may open with an opening sentence and the Invitatory. It may open with the Invitatory. No rubrical preference is given. The choice is a matter of personal taste.

Since the first prayer book in 1549, there have been many patterns to the prayers that follow the Collects. The PBCP provides significantly more flexibility, however, than its predecessors.

The simplest addition is the only one with a rubric requiring its use under defined circumstances. There are three prayers for mission after each Office. If no general intercessions are to be used, or if the Eucharist is not to follow, one of these prayers must be used. The alternative possibilities are very broad, however.

The rubric lists two possibilities: general intercession or the Eucharist. General intercessions may be found in three places: in a special section between pages 810 and 841, which includes a vast range of corporate and personal prayers and thanksgivings, and is cross-referenced to other specific prayers found elsewhere in the PBCP; in the Great Litany, which begins on page 148 and includes, as a special section, the Supplication, for use " . . . especially in time of war, or of national anxiety or of disaster"; in the intercessions designed for use with the Eucharist, called the Prayers of the People, which occur, in six forms, between pages 383 and 395 of the PBCP.

The existence of a number of books of prayers to supplement those available in the 1928 Prayer Book indicated a need for considerable supplementing of the available devotional material. In addition, because the Office printed specific prayers after the third Collect, they appeared to be the "official" prayers to be used in that spot. The other prayers available were less likely to be used. Part of that may have been a function of the lack of cross-reference and the existence of two section of prayers, one after the Offices, the other back in "Family Prayer." Whatever the cause, the revisers have collected all of the prayers in one place, insofar as possible, and have provided clear reference to the rest. For anyone planning to recite an Office, there is an index to the prayers (pages 810-813). Since the pattern in which they are printed more or less follows the list of what should be in a balanced intercession (which appears in conjunction with the Prayers of the People), any Officiant should have scant trouble in meeting his or her devotional needs. There are seventy prayers and eleven thanksgivings, plus references to material from elsewhere in the book. No study of the Office would be complete without a careful review of the section of Prayers and Thanksgivings.

In 1544, Archbishop Cranmer prepared the Great Litany. It preceded the first prayer book by five years, and was the first "official" liturgy in English. It is a credit to its flexibility that when, four hundred and thirty-two years after its publication, a new edition was offered, it varied only slightly from its progenitor. In the *Oxford American Prayer Book Commentary*, Dr. Massey Shepherd notes that "each successive revision of the Prayer Book has contributed some alterations to the Litany, whether by omission or addition, so that no other Office in the Prayer Book exhibits so masterful a combination of the manifold contributions of succeeding generations to the corporate prayer of the Church" (page 54). What was true of the 1928 edition is equally true of the 1976 edition. The introductory rubric to The Great Litany in the PBCP (page 148) notes that it may be used after the Collects of Morning or Evening Prayer. It further notes that it is especially appropriate in Lent and on the Rogation Days. For anyone reading the Office daily, the Litany is a particularly useful worship form to be recited regularly.

In the American prayer books, the later portion of the Litany has always been optional, although the exact cut-off point has varied. In the PBCP, however, the excised material has been moved to a separate position and retitled The Supplication. Its rubric (page 154) allows it to be used as an ending to the Litany, after the third Collect or separately. Certainly, in our uncertain times, war, anxiety and disaster are not unknown. Specific material for those occasions serves the purpose better than optional material in another service.

The Eucharist provides six intercessions, ranging in form from litanies to biddings to versicles and responses. They provide varying amounts of opportunity for specific mention of personal or communal need. They provide a more compact form of general intercession than the other alternatives, but a rather less particular or personal form.

When the Office is being recited publicly, not privately, there are two rubrics of importance. One, in the Office proper, permits the singing of a hymn or anthem after the Collects and before the general intercessions. The other, in Additional Directions on page 142, says that opportunity may be given for members of the congregation "to express intentions or objects of prayer and thanksgiving . . . and opportunity may be given for silent prayer."

When the prayer for mission or the general intercession has been used, there are four further choices, any or none of which may be used. These are: The General Thanksgiving; A Prayer of St. Chrysostom; a dismissal; closing passages of Scripture.

The General Thanksgiving and the Prayer of St. Chrysostom are substantially in the same place and same form to which we have long been accustomed. There are other forms of thanksgiving, general and specific, in the section of prayers and thanksgivings. The Prayer of St. Chrysostom can be considered as a kind of "summary collect" to end the prayer portion of the Office liturgy.

The addition to the customary material is the introduction of a dismissal. Although long known in rites of our sister communions, it has not been used much among Anglicans. Its use is now suggested in both Rites I and II of the Eucharist and in rites that will not be accompanied by a Eucharist. In the Office, the dismissal can be seen as a parallel to the Invitatory. One is a versicle and response that opens the rite, the other is a versicle and response that closes it.

By the same kind of logic, then, the Grace and the two other verses of Scripture that accompany it can be seen as a parallel to the opening sentences. The Office opens with a "call to worship" from Scripture. It closes with a scriptural doxology. By use of permissive rubrics, one may carry the parallel through, or one may ignore it.

Only one element remains to be discussed. The rubric on page 142 allows for a sermon either after the Office or within it. If it falls within, it comes either after the readings or following the music after the Collects. As has been noted earlier, if the Office is read privately, the place for the sermon is the place for a meditation. In either case, use of reflection, public or private, upon the meaning of Holy Scripture parallels the Eucharist when it follows immediately upon the conclusion of the readings. If such reflection does not take place after the readings, the end of the Office is affected. If the sermon or its substitute is positioned after the third Collect, then the latter portion of the Office will be composed of the prayers and thanksgivings, concluding with the Dismissal or Grace. If the sermon follows the close of the Office, then some additional material must be pieced in (as has customarily been true) to end the whole service. For private use, either of the former positions seems more appropriate. For public use, local and particular concerns need be considered which are not the province of this study.

It should be noted that the PBCP permits the use of the Office as that portion of the Eucharist that precedes the Offertory. In technical terms, that section of the rite is called the Proanaphora. In the PBCP that portion of the rite is called the Liturgy of the Word. The appropriate rubrics are on page 142 of PBCP under the general heading "When there is a Communion."

These rubrics permit the Office to be read in the usual fashion, requiring only that the Intercessions conform to the directions for the Intercessions at a Eucharist and that the optional endings be dropped and the service continue with the (Peace and) Offertory.

If, however, one wishes to conform the Office more closely to the Liturgy of the Word, one may substitute the Nicene for the Apostles' Creed, skip the Suffrages and Lord's Prayer and use only the Collect of the Day. Needless to say, one of the readings, under either use, must be from the Gospel.

The Office, then, is a liturgy of praise, Word and prayer. It is for use by the whole people of God, clergy and laity. It is designed to provide a foundation of Scripture for edification and inspiration. The proposed uses, whether Rite I or Rite II, whether read as two Offices or as a single daily Office, are designed to fulfill the goals for the Anglican Office that Archbishop Cranmer enunciated in 1549, including that of inflaming the faithful with the love of true religion.

Shorter Offices

In addition to the regular daily Office, the PBCP provides several shorter offices. These more closely resemble the monastic diurnal in pattern than the daily Office that Archbishop Cranmer developed. There are Offices for Noonday and Compline. In addition to these, there is an Order of Worship for the Evening, and a series of Daily Devotions for Individuals and Families.

The briefer Offices, in general, have a limited selection of Psalms, appropriate to the hour of the day, and a limited selection of "Short Lessons", usually one or two verses, also appropriate to the occasion. They provide a single Collect and opportunity for free intercessory prayer. Compline, which is the more complex of the two Offices, provides a confession and a Canticle as well.

The Daily Devotions "follow the basic structure of the Daily Office" (PBCP page 136), but are briefer. They replace Family Prayer in the 1928 book. The general rubrics on page 136 provide that the Office or Eucharistic lectionary may be used, as well as the appropriate Collect. Brief forms for Morning, Noon, Evening and Close of Day are provided. Any is complete in itself. Each is less formal and provides less variety than the regular daily Office. With use of the regular lectionary, however, each can provide that knowledge and inspiration from Scripture that Archbishop Cranmer considered so essential.

The Order for Evening is a different matter. It provides the setting for what, in the best sense, can be considered liturgical mixed media. It is a rite in which the ambience is an essential factor. The rubrics on page 142, as well as those on page 108, spell the matter out. The rite is not meant to stand alone, but as an introduction to some other form of activity. It begins like a short Office, with versicles and a Short Lesson. An appropriate Collect follows. All of this is done with the worship setting as dark as possible. After the Collect, the candles are lighted, and the worship area emerges into light. Appropriate music or silence are used during the lighting. The *Phos hilaron*, either as printed or in the *Hymnal* versions is used. Then, either the evening Office, the Eucharist or a sequence of Psalms, Scripture, Canticle, Prayers and Blessing/Dismissal follow. To increase the sense of mixed media, incense is suggested for use during the *Phos hilaron*.

Taken together with the daily Office, these addenda provide those using PBCP a full opportunity to make prayer and Scripture an integral part of day-to-day living. The section of PBCP listed as the Daily Office in the Table of Contents provides for short and long forms for individuals, congregations and families to recite the Office four times in the day. It provides for the sanctification of the Christian's time and activities. It serves as a constant reminder that God is not separate from any of the days of a Christian's life, nor from any of his or her activities. The pattern provided within the week and within the year provides a kind of structure upon which one may, by God's Grace, build the structure of one's sanctification. It is a way to offer the sorrow of a Friday and the expectancy of a Saturday, as well as the joy of a Sunday. It is the way to offer the penitence of Lent and the exultation of Easter. Because it provides for the offering of one's whole being, the Office becomes a way to "work out one's salvation with fear and trembling."

The Daily Office

Concerning the Service

In the Daily Office, the term "Officiant" is used to denote the person, clerical or lay, who leads the Office.

It is appropriate that other persons be assigned to read the Lessons, and to lead other parts of the service not assigned to the officiant. The bishop, when present, appropriately concludes the Office with a blessing.

At celebrations of the Holy Eucharist, the Order for Morning or Evening Prayer may be used in place of all that precedes the Offertory.

Additional Directions are on page 141.

Daily Morning Prayer: Rite One

The Officiant begins the service with one or more of these sentences of Scripture, or with the versicle "O Lord, open thou our lips" on page 42.

Advent

Watch ye, for ye know not when the master of the house cometh, at even, or at midnight, or at the cock-crowing, or in the morning; lest coming suddenly he find you sleeping. *Mark 13:35, 36*

Prepare ye the way of the Lord, make straight in the desert a highway for our God.   *Isaiah 40:3*

The glory of the Lord shall be revealed, and all flesh shall see it together.   *Isaiah 40:5*

Christmas

Behold, I bring you good tidings of great joy, which shall be to all people. For unto you is born this day in the city of David a Savior, which is Christ the Lord.   *Luke 2:10, 11*

Behold, the tabernacle of God is with men, and he will dwell with them, and they shall be his people, and God himself shall be with them, and be their God.   *Revelation 21:3*

Epiphany

The Gentiles shall come to thy light, and kings to the brightness of thy rising.   *Isaiah 60:3*

I will give thee for a light to the Gentiles, that thou mayest be my salvation unto the end of the earth.   *Isaiah 49:6b*

From the rising of the sun even unto the going down of the same my Name shall be great among the Gentiles, and in every place incense shall be offered unto my Name, and a pure offering: for my Name shall be great among the heathen, saith the Lord of hosts.   *Malachi 1:11*

Lent

If we say that we have no sin, we deceive ourselves, and the truth is not in us; but if we confess our sins, God is faithful and just to forgive us our sins, and to cleanse us from all unrighteousness.   *1 John 1:8, 9*

Rend your heart, and not your garments, and turn unto the Lord your God; for he is gracious and merciful, slow to anger and of great kindness, and repenteth him of the evil.   *Joel 2:13*

I will arise and go to my father, and will say unto him, "Father, I have sinned against heaven, and before thee, and am no more worthy to be called thy son."   *Luke 15:18, 19*

To the Lord our God belong mercies and forgivenesses, though we have rebelled against him; neither have we obeyed the voice of the Lord our God, to walk in his laws which he set before us.   *Daniel 9:9, 10*

Jesus said, "Whosoever will come after me, let him deny himself, and take up his cross, and follow me."   *Mark 8:34*

Holy Week

All we like sheep have gone astray; we have turned every one to his own way; and the Lord hath laid on him the iniquity of us all.   *Isaiah 53:6*

Is it nothing to you, all ye that pass by? Behold and see if there be any sorrow like unto my sorrow which is done unto me, wherewith the Lord hath afflicted me.   *Lamentations 1:12*

Easter Season, including Ascension Day and the Day of Pentecost

Alleluia! Christ is risen.
The Lord is risen indeed. Alleluia!

This is the day which the Lord hath made; we will rejoice and be glad in it.   *Psalm 118:24*

Thanks be to God, which giveth us the victory through our Lord Jesus Christ.   *1 Corinthians 15:57*

If ye then be risen with Christ, seek those things which are above, where Christ sitteth on the right hand of God.   *Colossians 3:1*

Christ is not entered into the holy places made with hands, which are the figures of the true; but into heaven itself, now to appear in the presence of God for us.   *Hebrews 9:24*

Ye shall receive power, after that the Holy Ghost is come upon you; and ye shall be witnesses unto me both in Jerusalem, and in all Judaea, and in Samaria, and unto the uttermost part of the earth.   *Acts 1:8*

Trinity Sunday

Holy, holy, holy, Lord God Almighty, which was, and is, and is to come.   *Revelation 4:8*

All Saints and other Major Saints' Days

We give thanks unto the Father, which hath made us meet to be partakers of the inheritance of the saints in light. *Colossians 1:12*

Ye are no more strangers and foreigners, but fellow-citizens with the saints and of the household of God.   *Ephesians 2:19*

Their sound is gone out into all lands; and their words into the ends of the world.   *Psalm 19:4*

Occasions of Thanksgiving

O give thanks unto the Lord, and call upon his Name; tell the people what things he hath done.   *Psalm 105:1*

At any Time

Grace be unto you, and peace, from God our Father, and from the Lord Jesus Christ.   *Philippians 1:2*

I was glad when they said unto me, "We will go into the house of the Lord."   *Psalm 122:1*

Let the words of my mouth, and the meditation of my heart, be alway acceptable in thy sight, O Lord, my strength and my redeemer.   *Psalm 19:14*

O send out thy light and thy truth, that they may lead me, and bring me unto thy holy hill, and to thy dwelling. *Psalm 43:3*

The Lord is in his holy temple; let all the earth keep silence before him.   *Habakkuk 2:20*

The hour cometh, and now is, when the true worshipers shall worship the Father in spirit and in truth; for the Father seeketh such to worship him.   *John 4:23*

Thus saith the high and lofty One that inhabiteth eternity,

whose name is Holy," I dwell in the high and holy place, with him also that is of a contrite and humble spirit, to revive the spirit of the humble, and to revive the heart of the contrite ones."   Isaiah 57:15

The following Confession of Sin may then be said; or the Office may continue at once with "O Lord, open thou our lips."

Confession of Sin

The Officiant says to the people

Dearly beloved, we have come together in the presence of Almighty God our heavenly Father, to render thanks for the great benefits that we have received at his hands, to set forth his most worthy praise, to hear his holy Word, and to ask, for ourselves and on behalf of others, those things that are necessary for our life and our salvation. And so that we may prepare ourselves in heart and mind to worship him, let us kneel in silence, and with penitent and obedient hearts confess our sins, that we may obtain forgiveness by his infinite goodness and mercy.

or this

Let us humbly confess our sins unto Almighty God.

Silence may be kept.

Officiant and People together, all kneeling

Almighty and most merciful Father,
we have erred and strayed from thy ways like lost sheep,
we have followed too much the devices and desires of our
    own hearts,
we have offended against thy holy laws,
we have left undone those things which we ought to
    have done,

and we have done those things which we ought not to
 have done.
But thou, O Lord, have mercy upon us,
spare thou those who confess their faults,
restore thou those who are penitent,
according to thy promises declared unto mankind
in Christ Jesus our Lord;
and grant, O most merciful Father, for his sake,
that we may hereafter live a godly, righteous, and sober life,
to the glory of thy holy Name. Amen.

The Priest alone stands and says

The Almighty and merciful Lord grant you absolution and remission of all your sins, true repentance, amendment of life, and the grace and consolation of his Holy Spirit. *Amen.*

A deacon or lay person using the preceding form remains kneeling, and substitutes "us" for "you" and "our" for "your."

The Invitatory and Psalter

All stand

Officiant   O Lord, open thou our lips.
People   And our mouth shall show forth thy praise.

Officiant and People

Glory to the Father, and to the Son, and to the Holy Spirit: as it was in the beginning, is now, and will be for ever. Amen.

Except in Lent,   Alleluia   *may be added.*

Then follows one of the Invitatory Psalms, Venite or Jubilate.

One of the following Antiphons may be sung or said with the Invitatory Psalm

In Advent

Our King and Savior draweth nigh: O come, let us adore him.

On the Twelve Days of Christmas

Alleluia. Unto us a child is born: O come, let us adore him. Alleluia.

From the Epiphany through the Baptism of Christ, and on the Feasts of the Transfiguration and Holy Cross

The Lord hath manifested forth his glory: O come, let us adore him.

In Lent

The Lord is full of compassion and mercy: O come, let us adore him.

From Easter Day until the Ascension

Alleluia. The Lord is risen indeed: O come, let us adore him. Alleluia.

From Ascension Day until the Day of Pentecost

Alleluia. Christ the Lord ascendeth into heaven: O come, let us adore him. Alleluia.

On the Day of Pentecost

Alleluia. The Spirit of the Lord filleth the world: O come, let us adore him. Alleluia.

On Trinity Sunday

Father, Son, and Holy Ghost, one God: O come, let us adore him.

On other Sundays and Weekdays

The earth is the Lord's for he made it: O come, let us adore him.

or this

Worship the Lord in the beauty of holiness: O come, let us adore him.

or this

The mercy of the Lord is everlasting: O come, let us adore him.

The Alleluias in the following Antiphons are used only in Easter Season.

On Feasts of the Incarnation

[Alleluia.] The Word was made flesh and dwelt among us: O come, let us adore him. [Alleluia.]

On All Saints and other Major Saints' Days

[Alleluia.] The Lord is glorious in his saints: O come, let us adore him. [Alleluia.]

Venite *Psalm 95:1-7; 96:9, 13*

O come, let us sing unto the Lord; *
    let us heartily rejoice in the strength of our salvation.
Let us come before his presence with thanksgiving, *
    and show ourselves glad in him with psalms.

For the Lord is a great God, *
    and a great King above all gods.
In his hand are all the corners of the earth, *
    and the strength of the hills is his also.
The sea is his and he made it, *
    and his hands prepared the dry land.

O come, let us worship and fall down *
  and kneel before the Lord our Maker.
For he is the Lord our God, *
  and we are the people of his pasture
  and the sheep of his hand.

O worship the Lord in the beauty of holiness; *
  let the whole earth stand in awe of him.
For he cometh, for he cometh to judge the earth, *
  and with righteousness to judge the world
  and the peoples with his truth.

or Psalm 95, page 146.

Jubilate   *Psalm 100*

O be joyful in the Lord all ye lands; *
  serve the Lord with gladness
  and come before his presence with a song.

Be ye sure that the Lord he is God;
it is he that hath made us and not we ourselves; *
  we are his people and the sheep of his pasture.

O go your way into his gates with thanksgiving
and into his courts with praise; *
  be thankful unto him and speak good of his Name.

For the Lord is gracious;
his mercy is everlasting; *
  and his truth endureth from generation to generation.

In Easter Week, in place of an Invitatory Psalm, the following is sung or said. It may also be used daily until the Day of Pentecost.

Morning Prayer I

Christ our Passover *Pascha nostrum*
1 Corinthians 5:7-8; Romans 6:9-11; 1 Corinthians 15:20-22

Alleluia.
Christ our Passover is sacrificed for us, *
　　therefore let us keep the feast,
Not with old leaven,
neither with the leaven of malice and wickedness, *
　　but with the unleavened bread of sincerity and truth. Alleluia.

Christ being raised from the dead dieth no more; *
　　death hath no more dominion over him.
For in that he died, he died unto sin once; *
　　but in that he liveth, he liveth unto God.
Likewise reckon ye also yourselves to be dead indeed unto sin, *
　　but alive unto God through Jesus Christ our Lord. Alleluia.

Christ is risen from the dead, *
　　and become the first fruits of them that slept.
For since by man came death, *
　　by man came also the resurrection of the dead.
For as in Adam all die, *
　　even so in Christ shall all be made alive. Alleluia.

Then follows

The Psalm or Psalms Appointed

At the end of the Psalms is sung or said

Glory to the Father, and to the Son, and to the Holy Spirit: *
　　as it was in the beginning, is now, and will be for ever. Amen.

The Lessons

One or two Lessons, as appointed, are read, the Reader first saying

A Reading (Lesson) from _____.
A citation giving chapter and verse may be added.

After each Lesson the Reader may say

    The Word of the Lord.
Answer   Thanks be to God.

Or the Reader may say   Here endeth the Lesson (Reading).

Silence may be kept after each Reading. One of the following Canticles, or one of those on pages 85-95 (Canticles 8-21), is sung or said after each Reading. If three Lessons are used, the Lesson from the Gospel is read after the second Canticle.

1 A Song of Creation *Benedicite, omnia opera Domini*
Song of the Three Young Men, 35-65

This Canticle may be shortened by omitting section II or III

I *Invocation*

O all ye works of the Lord, bless ye the Lord; *
  praise him and magnify him for ever.
O ye angels of the Lord, bless ye the Lord; *
  praise him and magnify him for ever.

II *The Cosmic Order*

O ye heavens, bless ye the Lord; *
  O ye waters that be above the firmament, bless ye the Lord;
O all ye powers of the Lord, bless ye the Lord; *
  praise him and magnify him for ever.

O ye sun and moon, bless ye the Lord; *
    O ye stars of heaven, bless ye the Lord;
O ye showers and dew, bless ye the Lord; *
    praise him and magnify him for ever.

O ye winds of God, bless ye the Lord; *
    O ye fire and heat, bless ye the Lord;
O ye winter and summer, bless ye the Lord; *
    praise him and magnify him for ever.

O ye dews and frosts, bless ye the Lord; *
    O ye frost and cold, bless ye the Lord;
O ye ice and snow, bless ye the Lord; *
    praise him and magnify him for ever.

O ye nights and days, bless ye the Lord; *
    O ye light and darkness, bless ye the Lord;
O ye lightnings and clouds, bless ye the Lord; *
    praise him and magnify him for ever.

III *The Earth and its Creatures*

O let the earth bless the Lord; *
    O ye mountains and hills, bless ye the Lord;
O all ye green things upon the earth, bless ye the Lord; *
    praise him and magnify him for ever.

O ye wells, bless ye the Lord; *
    O ye seas and floods, bless ye the Lord;
O ye whales and all that move in the waters, bless ye the Lord; *
    praise him and magnify him for ever.

O all ye fowls of the air, bless ye the Lord; *
    O all ye beasts and cattle, bless ye the Lord;
O ye children of men, bless ye the Lord; *
    praise him and magnify him for ever.

IV *The People of God*

O ye people of God, bless ye the Lord; *
  O ye priests of the Lord, bless ye the Lord;
O ye servants of the Lord, bless ye the Lord; *
  praise him and magnify him for ever.

O ye spirits and souls of the righteous, bless ye the Lord; *
  O ye holy and humble men of heart, bless ye the Lord.
Let us bless the Father, the Son, and the Holy Spirit; *
  praise him and magnify him for ever.

2 A Song of Praise   *Benedictus es, Domine*
Song of the Three Young Men, 29-34

Blessed art thou, O Lord God of our fathers; *
  praised and exalted above all for ever.
Blessed art thou for the Name of thy Majesty; *
  praised and exalted above all for ever.
Blessed art thou in the temple of thy holiness; *
  praised and exalted above all for ever.
Blessed art thou that beholdest the depths,
and dwellest between the Cherubim; *
  praised and exalted above all for ever.
Blessed art thou on the glorious throne of thy kingdom; *
  praised and exalted above all for ever.
Blessed art thou in the firmament of heaven; *
  praised and exalted above all for ever.
Blessed art thou, O Father, Son, and Holy Spirit; *
  praised and exalted above all for ever.

3   The Song of Mary   *Magnificat*
Luke 1:46-55

My soul doth magnify the Lord, *
 and my spirit hath rejoiced in God my Savior.
For he hath regarded *
 the lowliness of his handmaiden.
For behold from henceforth *
 all generations shall call me blessed.
For he that is mighty hath magnified me, *
 and holy is his Name.
And his mercy is on them that fear him *
 throughout all generations.
He hath showed strength with his arm; *
 he hath scattered the proud in the imagination of their hearts.
He hath put down the mighty from their seat, *
 and hath exalted the humble and meek.
He hath filled the hungry with good things, *
 and the rich he hath sent empty away.
He remembering his mercy hath holpen his servant Israel, *
 as he promised to our forefathers,
 Abraham and his seed for ever.

Glory to the Father, and to the Son, and to the Holy Spirit: *
 as it was in the beginning, is now, and will be for ever. Amen.

4   The Song of Zechariah   *Benedictus Dominus Deus*
Luke 1:68-79

Blessed be the Lord God of Israel, *
 for he hath visited and redeemed his people;
And hath raised up a mighty salvation for us *
 in the house of his servant David,
As he spake by the mouth of his holy prophets, *
 which have been since the world began:

That we should be saved from our enemies, *
    and from the hand of all that hate us;
To perform the mercy promised to our forefathers, *
    and to remember his holy covenant;
To perform the oath which he sware to our forefather Abraham, *
    that he would give us,
That we being delivered out of the hand of our enemies *
    might serve him without fear,
In holiness and righteousness before him, *
    all the days of our life.

And thou, child, shalt be called the prophet of the Highest, *
    for thou shalt go before the face of the Lord
    to prepare his ways;
To give knowledge of salvation unto his people *
    for the remission of their sins,
Through the tender mercy of our God, *
    whereby the dayspring from on high hath visited us;
To give light to them that sit in darkness
and in the shadow of death, *
    and to guide our feet into the way of peace.

Glory to the Father, and to the Son, and to the Holy Spirit: *
    as it was in the beginning, is now, and will be for ever. Amen.

5   The Song of Simeon   *Nunc dimittis*
Luke 2:29-32

Lord, now lettest thou thy servant depart in peace, *
    according to thy word;
For mine eyes have seen thy salvation, *
    which thou hast prepared before the face of all people,
To be a light to lighten the Gentiles, *
    and to be the glory of thy people Israel.

Glory to the Father, and to the Son, and to the Holy Spirit: *
   as it was in the beginning, is now, and will be for ever. Amen.

6   Glory be to God   *Gloria in excelsis*

Glory be to God on high,
   and on earth peace, good will towards men.

We praise thee, we bless thee,
   we worship thee,
   we glorify thee,
   we give thanks to thee for thy great glory,
O Lord God, heavenly King, God the Father Almighty.

O Lord, the only-begotten Son, Jesus Christ;
O Lord God, Lamb of God, Son of the Father,
   that takest away the sins of the world,
      have mercy upon us.
Thou that takest away the sins of the world,
   receive our prayer.
Thou that sittest at the right hand of God the Father,
   have mercy upon us.

For thou only art holy,
thou only art the Lord,
thou only, O Christ,
   with the Holy Ghost,
   art most high in the glory of God the Father. Amen.

7   We Praise Thee   *Te Deum laudamus*

We praise thee, O God; we acknowledge thee to be the Lord.
All the earth doth worship thee, the Father everlasting.
To thee all Angels cry aloud,
   the Heavens and all the Powers therein.
To thee Cherubim and Seraphim continually do cry:

Holy, holy, holy, Lord God of Sabaoth;
   Heaven and earth are full of the majesty of thy glory.
The glorious company of the apostles praise thee.
The goodly fellowship of the prophets praise thee.
The noble army of martyrs praise thee.
The holy Church throughout all the world
                 doth acknowledge thee,
  the Father, of an infinite majesty,
  thine adorable, true, and only Son,
  also the Holy Ghost the Comforter.

Thou art the King of glory, O Christ.
Thou art the everlasting Son of the Father.
When thou tookest upon thee to deliver man,
thou didst humble thyself to be born of a Virgin.
When thou hadst overcome the sharpness of death,
thou didst open the kingdom of heaven to all believers.
Thou sittest at the right hand of God, in the glory of the Father.
We believe that thou shalt come to be our judge.
  We therefore pray thee, help thy servants,
  whom thou hast redeemed with thy precious blood.
  Make them to be numbered with thy saints,
  in glory everlasting.

The Apostles' Creed

Officiant and People together, all standing

I believe in God, the Father almighty,
  maker of heaven and earth;
And in Jesus Christ his only Son our Lord;
  who was conceived by the Holy Ghost,
  born of the Virgin Mary,
  suffered under Pontius Pilate,
  was crucified, dead, and buried.
  He descended into hell.

The third day he rose again from the dead.
He ascended into heaven,
    and sitteth on the right hand of God the Father almighty.
    From thence he shall come to judge the quick and the dead.
I believe in the Holy Ghost,
    the holy catholic Church,
    the communion of saints,
    the forgiveness of sins,
    the resurrection of the body,
    and the life everlasting. Amen.

The text of the Creed on page 96 may be used instead.

The Prayers

The people stand or kneel

Officiant   The Lord be with you.
People   And with thy spirit.
Officiant   Let us pray.

Officiant and People

Our Father, who art in heaven,
    hallowed be thy Name,
    thy kingdom come,
    thy will be done,
        on earth as it is in heaven.
Give us this day our daily bread.
And forgive us our trespasses,
    as we forgive those who trespass against us.
And lead us not into temptation,
    but deliver us from evil.
For thine is the kingdom, and the power, and the glory,
    for ever and ever. Amen.

Then follows one of these sets of Suffrages

A

V. O Lord, show thy mercy upon us;
R. And grant us thy salvation.
V. Endue thy ministers with righteousness;
R. And make thy chosen people joyful.
V. Give peace, O Lord, in all the world;
R. For only in thee can we live in safety.
V. Lord, keep this nation under thy care;
R. And guide us in the way of justice and truth.
V. Let thy way be known upon earth;
R. Thy saving health among all nations.
V. Let not the needy, O Lord, be forgotten;
R. Nor the hope of the poor be taken away.
V. Create in us clean hearts, O God;
R. And sustain us with thy Holy Spirit.

B

V. O Lord, save thy people, and bless thine heritage;
R. Govern them and lift them up for ever.
V. Day by day we magnify thee;
R. And we worship thy Name ever, world without end.
V. Vouchsafe, O Lord, to keep us this day without sin;
R. O Lord, have mercy upon us, have mercy upon us.
V. O Lord, let thy mercy be upon us;
R. As our trust is in thee.
V. O Lord, in thee have I trusted;
R. Let me never be confounded.

The Officiant then says one or more of the following Collects

The Collect of the Day

A Collect for Sundays

O God, who makest us glad with the weekly remembrance of the glorious resurrection of thy Son our Lord: Grant us this day such blessing through our worship of thee, that the days to come may be spent in thy favor; through the same Jesus Christ our Lord. *Amen.*

A Collect for Fridays

Almighty God, whose most dear Son went not up to joy but first he suffered pain, and entered not into glory before he was crucified: Mercifully grant that we, walking in the way of the cross, may find it none other than the way of life and peace; through the same thy Son Jesus Christ our Lord. *Amen.*

A Collect for Saturdays

Almighty God, who after the creation of the world didst rest from all thy works and sanctify a day of rest for all thy creatures: Grant that we, putting away all earthly anxieties, may be duly prepared for the service of thy sanctuary, and that our rest here upon earth may be a preparation for the eternal rest promised to thy people in heaven; through Jesus Christ our Lord. *Amen.*

A Collect for the Renewal of Life

O God, the King eternal, who dividest the day from the night and turnest the shadow of death into the morning: Drive far from us all wrong desires, incline our hearts to keep thy law, and guide our feet into the way of peace; that, having done thy will with cheerfulness while it was day, we may, when the night cometh, rejoice to give thee thanks; through Jesus Christ our Lord. *Amen.*

A Collect for Peace

O God, who art the author of peace and lover of concord, in knowledge of whom standeth our eternal life, whose service is perfect freedom: Defend us, thy humble servants, in all assaults of our enemies; that we, surely trusting in thy defense, may not fear the power of any adversaries; through the might of Jesus Christ our Lord. *Amen.*

A Collect for Grace

O Lord, our heavenly Father, almighty and everlasting God, who hast safely brought us to the beginning of this day: Defend us in the same with thy mighty power; and grant that this day we fall into no sin, neither run into any kind of danger; but that we, being ordered by thy governance, may do always what is righteous in thy sight; through Jesus Christ our Lord. *Amen.*

A Collect for Guidance

O heavenly Father, in whom we live and move and have our being: We humbly pray thee so to guide and govern us by thy Holy Spirit, that in all the cares and occupations of our life we may not forget thee, but may remember that we are ever walking in thy sight; through Jesus Christ our Lord. *Amen.*

Then, unless the Eucharist or a form of general intercession is to follow, one of these prayers for mission is added

Almighty and everlasting God, by whose Spirit the whole body of thy faithful people is governed and sanctified: Receive our supplications and prayers which we offer before thee for all members of thy holy Church, that in their vocation and ministry they may truly and godly serve thee; through our Lord and Savior Jesus Christ. *Amen.*

or the following

O God, who hast made of one blood all the peoples of the earth, and didst send thy blessed Son to preach peace to those who are far off and to those who are near: Grant that people everywhere may seek after thee and find thee; bring the nations into thy fold; pour out thy Spirit upon all flesh; and hasten the coming of thy kingdom; through the same thy Son Jesus Christ our Lord. *Amen.*

or this

Lord Jesus Christ, who didst stretch out thine arms of love on the hard wood of the cross that everyone might come within the reach of thy saving embrace: So clothe us in thy Spirit that we, reaching forth our hands in love, may bring those who do not know thee to the knowledge and love of thee; for the honor of thy Name. *Amen.*

Here may be sung a hymn or anthem.

Authorized intercessions and thanksgivings may follow.

Before the close of the Office one or both of the following may be used

The General Thanksgiving

Officiant and People

Almighty God, Father of all mercies,
we thine unworthy servants
do give thee most humble and hearty thanks
for all thy goodness and loving-kindness
to us and to all men.
We bless thee for our creation, preservation,
and all the blessings of this life;
but above all for thine inestimable love
in the redemption of the world by our Lord Jesus Christ,
for the means of grace, and for the hope of glory.

And, we beseech thee,
give us that due sense of all thy mercies,
that our hearts may be unfeignedly thankful;
and that we show forth thy praise,
not only with our lips, but in our lives,
by giving up our selves to thy service,
and by walking before thee
in holiness and righteousness all our days;
through Jesus Christ our Lord,
to whom, with thee and the Holy Ghost,
be all honor and glory, world without end. Amen.

A Prayer of St. Chrysostom

Almighty God, who hast given us grace at this time with one accord to make our common supplication unto thee, and hast promised through thy well-beloved Son that when two or three are gathered together in his Name thou wilt be in the midst of them: Fulfill now, O Lord, the desires and petitions of thy servants as may be best for us; granting us in this world knowledge of thy truth, and in the world to come life everlasting. *Amen.*

Then may be said

Let us bless the Lord.
Thanks be to God.

From Easter Day through the Day of Pentecost "Alleluia, alleluia" may be added to the preceding versicle and response.

The Officiant may then conclude with one of the following

The grace of our Lord Jesus Christ, and the love of God, and the fellowship of the Holy Ghost, be with us all evermore. *Amen.*   2 *Corinthians 13:14*

May the God of hope fill us with all joy and peace in believing through the power of the Holy Spirit. *Amen.*
Romans 15:13

Glory to God whose power, working in us, can do infinitely more than we can ask or imagine: Glory to him from generation to generation in the Church, and in Christ Jesus for ever and ever. *Amen.*   *Ephesians 3:20, 21*

Daily Evening Prayer: Rite One

The Officiant begins the service with one or more of the following sentences of Scripture, or of those on pages 37-40;

or with the Service of Light on pages 109-112, and continuing with the appointed Psalmody;

or with the versicle "O God, make speed to save us" on page 63.

Let my prayer be set forth in thy sight as the incense, and let the lifting up of my hands be an evening sacrifice.
Psalm 141:2

Grace be unto you, and peace, from God our Father, and from the Lord Jesus Christ.   *Philippians 1:2*

O worship the Lord in the beauty of holiness; let the whole earth stand in awe of him.   *Psalm 96:9*

Thine is the day, O God, thine also the night; thou hast established the moon and the sun. Thou hast fixed all the boundaries of the earth; thou hast made summer and winter.
Psalm 74:15, 16

I will bless the Lord who giveth me counsel; my heart teacheth me, night after night. I have set the Lord always before me; because he is at my right hand, I shall not fall.
Psalm 16:7, 8

Seek him that made the Pleiades and Orion, that turneth deep darkness into the morning, and darkeneth the day into night; that calleth for the waters of the sea, and poureth them out upon the face of the earth: The Lord is his Name. *Amos 5:8*

If I say, "Surely the darkness will cover me, and the light around me turn to night," darkness is not dark to thee, O Lord; the night is as bright as the day; darkness and light to thee are both alike. *Psalm 139:10, 11*

Jesus said, "I am the light of the world; he that followeth me shall not walk in darkness, but shall have the light of life." *John 8:12*

The following Confession of Sin may then be said; or the Office may continue at once with "O God make speed to save us."

Confession of Sin

The Officiant says to the people

Dear friends in Christ, here in the presence of Almighty God, let us kneel in silence, and with penitent and obedient hearts confess our sins, so that we may obtain forgiveness by his infinite goodness and mercy.

or this

Let us humbly confess our sins unto Almighty God.

Silence may be kept.

Officiant and People together, all kneeling

Almighty and most merciful Father,
we have erred and strayed from thy ways like lost sheep,
we have followed too much the devices and desires of our
    own hearts,

we have offended against thy holy laws,
we have left undone those things which we ought to
 have done,
and we have done those things which we ought not to
 have done.
But thou, O Lord, have mercy upon us,
spare thou those who confess their faults,
restore thou those who are penitent,
according to thy promises declared unto mankind
in Christ Jesus our Lord;
and grant, O most merciful Father, for his sake,
that we may hereafter live a godly, righteous, and sober life,
to the glory of thy holy Name. Amen.

The Priest alone stands and says

The Almighty and merciful Lord grant you absolution and remission of all your sins, true repentance, amendment of life, and the grace and consolation of his Holy Spirit. *Amen.*

A deacon or lay person using the preceding form remains kneeling, and substitutes "us" for "you" and "our" for "your."

The Invitatory and Psalter

All stand

Officiant O God, make speed to save us.
People O Lord, make haste to help us.

Officiant and People

Glory to the Father, and to the Son, and to the Holy Spirit: as it was in the beginning, is now, and will be for ever. Amen.

Except in Lent, Alleluia *may be added.*

The following, or some other suitable hymn, or an Invitatory Psalm, may be sung or said

O Gracious Light *Phos hilaron*

O gracious Light,
pure brightness of the everliving Father in heaven,
O Jesus Christ, holy and blessed!

Now as we come to the setting of the sun,
and our eyes behold the vesper light,
we sing thy praises, O God: Father, Son, and Holy Spirit.

Thou art worthy at all times to be praised by happy voices,
O Son of God, O Giver of life,
and to be glorified through all the worlds.

Then follows

The Psalm or Psalms Appointed

At the end of the Psalms is sung or said

Glory to the Father, and to the Son, and to the Holy Spirit: *
    as it was in the beginning, is now, and will be for ever. Amen

The Lessons

One or two Lessons, as appointed, are read, the Reader first saying

A Reading (Lesson) from _____.

A citation giving chapter and verse may be added.

After each Lesson the Reader may say

    The Word of the Lord.
Answer   Thanks be to God.

Or the Reader may say   Here endeth the Lesson (Reading).

Silence may be kept after each Reading. One of the following Canticles, or one of those on pages 47-52, or 85-95, is sung or said after each Reading. If three Lessons are used, the Lesson from the Gospel is read after the second Canticle.

The Song of Mary   *Magnificat*
Luke 1:46-55

My soul doth magnify the Lord, *
    and my spirit hath rejoiced in God my Savior.
For he hath regarded *
    the lowliness of his handmaiden.
For behold from henceforth *
    all generations shall call me blessed.
For he that is mighty hath magnified me, *
    and holy is his Name.
And his mercy is on them that fear him *
    throughout all generations.
He hath showed strength with his arm; *
    he hath scattered the proud in the imagination of their hearts.
He hath put down the mighty from their seat, *
    and hath exalted the humble and meek.
He hath filled the hungry with good things, *
    and the rich he hath sent empty away.
He remembering his mercy hath holpen his servant Israel, *
    as he promised to our forefathers,
    Abraham and his seed for ever.

Glory to the Father, and to the Son, and to the Holy Spirit: *
    as it was in the beginning, is now, and will be for ever. Amen.

The Song of Simeon *Nunc dimittis*
Luke 2:29-32

Lord, now lettest thou thy servant depart in peace, *
   according to thy word;
For mine eyes have seen thy salvation, *
   which thou hast prepared before the face of all people,
To be a light to lighten the Gentiles, *
   and to be the glory of thy people Israel.

Glory to the Father, and to the Son, and to the Holy Spirit: *
   as it was in the beginning, is now, and will be for ever. Amen.

The Apostles' Creed

Officiant and People together, all standing

I believe in God, the Father almighty,
   maker of heaven and earth;
And in Jesus Christ his only Son our Lord;
   who was conceived by the Holy Ghost,
   born of the Virgin Mary,
   suffered under Pontius Pilate,
   was crucified, dead, and buried..
   He descended into hell.
   The third day he rose again from the dead.
   He ascended into heaven,
   and sitteth on the right hand of God the Father almighty.
   From thence he shall come to judge the quick and the dead.
I believe in the Holy Ghost,
   the holy catholic Church,
   the communion of saints,
   the forgiveness of sins,
   the resurrection of the body,
   and the life everlasting. Amen.

The text of the Creed on page 120 may be used instead.

The Prayers

The people stand or kneel

Officiant The Lord be with you.
People   And with thy spirit.
Officiant Let us pray.

Officiant and People

Our Father, who art in heaven,
    hallowed be thy Name,
    thy kingdom come,
    thy will be done,
        on earth as it is in heaven.
Give us this day our daily bread.
And forgive us our trespasses,
    as we forgive those who trespass against us.
And lead us not into temptation,
    but deliver us from evil.
For thine is the kingdom, and the power, and the glory,
    for ever and ever. Amen.

Then follows one of these sets of Suffrages

A

V. O Lord, show thy mercy upon us;
R. And grant us thy salvation.
V. Endue thy ministers with righteousness;
R. And make thy chosen people joyful.
V. Give peace, O Lord, in all the world;
R. For only in thee can we live in safety.
V. Lord, keep this nation under thy care;
R. And guide us in the way of justice and truth.

V. Let thy way be known upon earth;
R. Thy saving health among all nations.
V. Let not the needy, O Lord, be forgotten;
R. Nor the hope of the poor be taken away.
V. Create in us clean hearts, O God;
R. And sustain us with thy Holy Spirit.

B

That this evening may be holy, good, and peaceful,
We entreat thee, O Lord.

That thy holy angels may lead us in paths of peace and goodwill,
We entreat thee, O Lord.

That we may be pardoned and forgiven for our sins and offenses,
We entreat thee, O Lord.

That there may be peace to thy Church and to the whole world,
We entreat thee, O Lord.

That we may depart this life in thy faith and fear, and not be condemned before the great judgment seat of Christ,
We entreat thee, O Lord.

That we may be bound together by thy Holy Spirit in the communion of [_____ and] all thy saints, entrusting one another and all our life to Christ,
We entreat thee, O Lord.

The Officiant then says one or more of the following Collects

The Collect of the Day

A Collect for Sundays

Lord God, whose Son our Savior Jesus Christ triumphed over the powers of death and prepared for us our place in the new Jerusalem: Grant that we, who have this day given thanks for his resurrection, may praise thee in that City of which he is the light; and where he liveth and reigneth for ever and ever. *Amen.*

A Collect for Fridays

O Lord Jesus Christ, who by thy death didst take away the sting of death: Grant unto us thy servants so to follow in faith where thou hast led the way, that we may at length fall asleep peacefully in thee, and awake up after thy likeness; for thy tender mercies' sake. *Amen.*

A Collect for Saturdays

O God, the source of eternal light: Shed forth thine unending day upon us who watch for thee, that our lips may praise thee, our lives may bless thee, and our worship on the morrow may give thee glory; through Jesus Christ our Lord. *Amen.*

A Collect for Peace

O God, from whom all holy desires, all good counsels, and all just works do proceed: Give unto thy servants that peace which the world cannot give, that our hearts may be set to obey thy commandments, and also that by thee, we, being defended from the fear of all enemies, may pass our time in rest and quietness; through the merits of Jesus Christ our Savior. *Amen.*

A Collect for Aid against Perils

Lighten our darkness, we beseech thee, O Lord; and by thy great mercy defend us from all perils and dangers of this night; for the love of thy only Son, our Savior Jesus Christ. *Amen.*

A Collect for Protection

O God, who art the life of all who live, the light of the faithful, the strength of those who labor, and the repose of the dead: We thank thee for the timely blessings of the day, and humbly beseech thy merciful protection all the night. Bring us, we pray thee, in safety to the morning hours; through him who died for us and rose again, thy Son our Savior Jesus Christ. *Amen.*

A Collect for the Presence of Christ

Lord Jesus, stay with us, for evening is at hand and the day is past; be our companion in the way, kindle our hearts, and awaken hope, that we may know thee as thou art revealed in Scripture and the breaking of bread. Grant this for the sake of thy love. *Amen.*

Then, unless the Eucharist or a form of general intercession is to follow, one of these prayers for mission is added

O God and Father of all, whom the whole heavens adore: Let the whole earth also worship thee, all nations obey thee, all tongues confess and bless thee, and men and women everywhere love thee and serve thee in peace; through Jesus Christ our Lord. *Amen.*

or the following

Keep watch, dear Lord, with those who work, or watch, or weep this night, and give thine angels charge over those who sleep. Tend the sick, Lord Christ; give rest to the weary, bless the dying, soothe the suffering, pity the afflicted, shield the joyous; and all for thy love's sake. *Amen.*

or this

O God, who dost manifest in thy servants the signs of thy presence: Send forth upon us the Spirit of love, that in companionship with one another thine abounding grace may increase among us; through Jesus Christ our Lord. *Amen.*

Here may be sung a hymn or anthem.

Authorized intercessions and thanksgivings may follow.

Before the close of the Office one or both of the following may be used

The General Thanksgiving

Officiant and People

Almighty God, Father of all mercies,
we thine unworthy servants
do give thee most humble and hearty thanks
for all thy goodness and loving-kindness
to us and to all men.
We bless thee for our creation, preservation,
and all the blessings of this life;
but above all for thine inestimable love
in the redemption of the world by our Lord Jesus Christ,
for the means of grace, and for the hope of glory.
And, we beseech thee,
give us that due sense of all thy mercies,
that our hearts may be unfeignedly thankful;

and that we show forth thy praise,
not only with our lips, but in our lives,
by giving up our selves to thy service,
and by walking before thee
in holiness and righteousness all our days;
through Jesus Christ our Lord,
to whom, with thee and the Holy Ghost,
be all honor and glory, world without end. Amen.

A Prayer of St. Chrysostom

Almighty God, who hast given us grace at this time with one accord to make our common supplication unto thee, and hast promised through thy well-beloved Son that when two or three are gathered together in his Name thou wilt be in the midst of them: Fulfill now, O Lord, the desires and petitions of thy servants as may be best for us; granting us in this world knowledge of thy truth, and in the world to come life everlasting. *Amen.*

Then may be said

Let us bless the Lord.
Thanks be to God.

From Easter Day through the Day of Pentecost "Alleluia, alleluia" may be added to the preceding versicle and response.

The Officiant may then conclude with one of the following

The grace of our Lord Jesus Christ, and the love of God, and the fellowship of the Holy Ghost, be with us all evermore. *Amen.*   2 *Corinthians* 13:14

May the God of hope fill us with all joy and peace in believing through the power of the Holy Spirit. *Amen.*
Romans 15:13

Glory to God whose power, working in us, can do infinitely more than we can ask or imagine: Glory to him from generation to generation in the Church, and in Christ Jesus for ever and ever. *Amen.*   *Ephesians 3:20, 21*

Concerning the Service

In the Daily Office, the term "Officiant" is used to denote the person, clerical or lay, who leads the Office.

It is appropriate that other persons be assigned to read the Lessons, and to lead other parts of the service not assigned to the officiant. The bishop, when present, appropriately concludes the Office with a blessing.

At celebrations of the Holy Eucharist, the Order for Morning or Evening Prayer may be used in place of all that precedes the Offertory.

Additional Directions are on page 141.

Daily Morning Prayer: Rite Two

The Officiant begins the service with one or more of these sentences of Scripture, or with the versicle "Lord, open our lips" on page 80.

Advent

Watch, for you do not know when the master of the house will come, in the evening, or at midnight, or at cockcrow, or in the morning, lest he come suddenly and find you asleep.   *Mark 13:35, 36*

In the wilderness prepare the way of the Lord, make straight in the desert a highway for our God.   *Isaiah 40:3*

The glory of the Lord shall be revealed, and all flesh shall see it together.   *Isaiah 40:5*

Christmas

Behold, I bring you good news of a great joy which will come to all the people; for to you is born this day in the city of David, a Savior, who is Christ the Lord.   *Luke 2:10, 11*

Behold, the dwelling of God is with mankind. He will dwell with them, and they shall be his people, and God himself will be with them, and be their God.   *Revelation 21:3*

Epiphany

Nations shall come to your light, and kings to the brightness of your rising.   *Isaiah 60:3*

I will give you as a light to the nations, that my salvation may reach to the end of the earth.   *Isaiah 49:6b*

From the rising of the sun to its setting my Name shall be great among the nations, and in every place incense shall be offered to my Name, and a pure offering; for my Name shall be great among the nations, says the Lord of hosts.   *Malachi 1:11*

Lent

If we say we have no sin, we deceive ourselves, and the truth is not in us, but if we confess our sins, God, who is faithful and just, will forgive our sins and cleanse us from all unrighteousness.   *1 John 1:8, 9*

Rend your hearts and not your garments. Return to the Lord your God, for he is gracious and merciful, slow to anger and abounding in steadfast love, and repents of evil.   *Joel 2:13*

I will arise and go to my father, and I will say to him, "Father, I have sinned against heaven and before you; I am no longer worthy to be called your son."   *Luke 15:18, 19*

To the Lord our God belong mercy and forgiveness, because we have rebelled against him and have not obeyed the voice of the Lord our God by following his laws which he set before us.   *Daniel 9:9, 10*

Jesus said,"If anyone would come after me, let him deny himself and take up his cross and follow me."   *Mark 8:34*

Holy Week

All we like sheep have gone astray; we have turned every one to his own way; and the Lord has laid on him the iniquity of us all.   *Isaiah 53:6*

Is it nothing to you, all you who pass by? Look and see if there is any sorrow like my sorrow which was brought upon me, whom the Lord has afflicted.   *Lamentations 1:12*

*Easter Season, including Ascension Day
and the Day of Pentecost*

Alleluia! Christ is risen.
The Lord is risen indeed. Alleluia!

On this day the Lord has acted; we will rejoice and be glad in it.   *Psalm 118:24*

Thanks be to God, who gives us the victory through our Lord Jesus Christ.   *1 Corinthians 15:57*

If then you have been raised with Christ, seek the things that are above, where Christ is, seated at the right hand of God.
Colossians 3:1

Christ has entered, not into a sanctuary made with hands, a copy of the true one, but into heaven itself, now to appear in the presence of God on our behalf.   *Hebrews 9:24*

You shall receive power when the Holy Spirit has come upon you; and you shall be my witnesses in Jerusalem, and in all Judea, and Samaria, and to the ends of the earth.   *Acts 1:8*

Trinity Sunday

Holy, holy, holy is the Lord God Almighty, who was, and is, and is to come!   *Revelation 4:8*

All Saints and other Major Saints' Days

We give thanks to the Father, who has made us worthy to share in the inheritance of the saints in light.   *Colossians 1:12*

You are no longer strangers and sojourners, but fellow citizens with the saints and members of the household of God.   *Ephesians 2:19*

Their sound has gone out into all lands, and their message to the ends of the world.   *Psalm 19:4*

Occasions of Thanksgiving

Give thanks to the Lord, and call upon his Name; make known his deeds among the peoples.   *Psalm 105:1*

At any Time

Grace to you and peace from God our Father and the Lord Jesus Christ.   *Philippians 1:2*

I was glad when they said to me, "Let us go to the house of the Lord."   *Psalm 122:1*

Let the words of my mouth and the meditation of my heart be acceptable in your sight, O Lord, my strength and my redeemer.   *Psalm 19:14*

Send out your light and your truth, that they may lead me, and bring me to your holy hill and to your dwelling.   *Psalm 43:3*

The Lord is in his holy temple; let all the earth keep silence before him.   *Habakkuk 2:20*

The hour is coming, and now is, when the true worshipers will worship the Father in spirit and truth, for such the Father seeks to worship him.   *John 4:23*

Thus says the high and lofty One who inhabits eternity, whose name is Holy, "I dwell in the high and holy place and also with the one who has a contrite and humble spirit, to revive the spirit of the humble and to revive the heart of the contrite."   *Isaiah 57:15*

The following Confession of Sin may then be said; or the Office may continue at once with "Lord, open our lips."

Confession of Sin

The Officiant says to the people

Dearly beloved, we have come together in the presence of Almighty God our heavenly Father, to set forth his praise, to hear his holy Word, and to ask, for ourselves and on behalf of others, those things that are necessary for our life and our salvation. And so that we may prepare ourselves in heart and mind to worship him, let us kneel in silence, and with penitent and obedient hearts confess our sins, that we may obtain forgiveness by his infinite goodness and mercy.

or this

Let us confess our sins against God and our neighbor.

Silence may be kept.

Officiant and People together, all kneeling

Most merciful God,
we confess that we have sinned against you
in thought, word, and deed,
by what we have done,
and by what we have left undone.
We have not loved you with our whole heart;
we have not loved our neighbors as ourselves.
We are truly sorry and we humbly repent.
For the sake of your Son Jesus Christ,
have mercy on us and forgive us;
that we may delight in your will,
and walk in your ways,
to the glory of your Name. Amen.

The Priest alone stands and says

Almighty God have mercy on you, forgive you all your sins through our Lord Jesus Christ, strengthen you in all goodness, and by the power of the Holy Spirit keep you in eternal life. *Amen.*

A deacon or lay person using the preceding form remains kneeling, and substitutes "us" for "you" and "our" for "your."

The Invitatory and Psalter

All stand

Officiant Lord, open our lips.
People   And our mouth shall proclaim your praise.

Officiant and People

Glory to the Father, and to the Son, and to the Holy Spirit: as it was in the beginning, is now, and will be for ever. Amen.

Except in Lent, add Alleluia.

Then follows one of the Invitatory Psalms, Venite or Jubilate.

One of the following Antiphons may be sung or said with the Invitatory Psalm

In Advent

Our King and Savior now draws near: Come let us adore him.

In Christmas Season

Alleluia. To us a child is born: Come let us adore him. Alleluia.

From the Epiphany through the Baptism of Christ, and on the Feasts of the Transfiguration and Holy Cross

The Lord has shown forth his glory: Come let us adore him.

In Lent

The Lord is full of compassion and mercy: Come let us adore him.

From Easter Day until the Ascension

Alleluia. The Lord is risen indeed: Come let us adore him. Alleluia.

From Ascension Day until the Day of Pentecost

Alleluia. Christ the Lord has ascended into heaven: Come let us adore him. Alleluia.

On the Day of Pentecost

Alleluia. The Spirit of the Lord renews the face of the earth: Come let us adore him. Alleluia.

On Trinity Sunday

Father, Son, and Holy Spirit, one God: Come let us adore him.

On other Sundays and weekdays

The earth is the Lord's, for he made it: Come let us adore him.

or this

Worship the Lord in the beauty of holiness: Come let us adore him.

or this

The mercy of the Lord is everlasting: Come let us adore him.

The Alleluias in the following Antiphons are used only in Easter Season.

On Feasts of the Incarnation

[Alleluia.] The Word was made flesh and dwelt among us: Come let us adore him. [Alleluia.]

On All Saints and other Major Saints' Days

[Alleluia.] The Lord is glorious in his saints: Come let us adore him. [Alleluia.]

Venite   *Psalm 95:1-7*

Come, let us sing to the Lord; *
    let us shout for joy to the Rock of our salvation.
Let us come before his presence with thanksgiving *
    and raise a loud shout to him with psalms.

For the Lord is a great God, *
    and a great King above all gods.
In his hand are the caverns of the earth, *
    and the heights of the hills are his also.
The sea is his, for he made it, *
    and his hands have molded the dry land.

Come, let us bow down, and bend the knee, *
    and kneel before the Lord our Maker.
For he is our God,
and we are the people of his pasture and the sheep of his hand.
    Oh, that today you would hearken to his voice!

or Psalm 95, page 724.

Jubilate   *Psalm 100*

Be joyful in the Lord, all you lands; *
    serve the Lord with gladness
    and come before his presence with a song.

Know this: The Lord himself is God; *
    he himself has made us, and we are his;
    we are his people and the sheep of his pasture.

Enter his gates with thanksgiving;
go into his courts with praise; *
    give thanks to him and call upon his Name.

For the Lord is good;
his mercy is everlasting; *
    and his faithfulness endures from age to age.

In Easter Week, in place of an Invitatory Psalm, the following is sung or said. It may also be used daily until the Day of Pentecost.

Christ our Passover   *Pascha nostrum*

1 Corinthians 5:7-8; Romans 6:9-11; 1 Corinthians 15:20-22

Alleluia.
Christ our Passover has been sacrificed for us; *
    therefore let us keep the feast,
Not with the old leaven, the leaven of malice and evil, *
    but with the unleavened bread of sincerity and truth. Alleluia.

Christ being raised from the dead will never die again; *
    death no longer has dominion over him.
The death that he died, he died to sin, once for all; *
    but the life he lives, he lives to God.
So also consider yourselves dead to sin, *
    and alive to God in Jesus Christ our Lord. Alleluia.

Christ has been raised from the dead, *
    the first fruits of those who have fallen asleep.
For since by a man came death, *
    by a man has come also the resurrection of the dead.
For as in Adam all die, *
    so also in Christ shall all be made alive. Alleluia.

Then follows

The Psalm or Psalms Appointed

At the end of the Psalms is sung or said

Glory to the Father, and to the Son, and to the Holy Spirit: *
 as it was in the beginning, is now, and will be for ever. Amen.

The Lessons

One or two Lessons, as appointed, are read, the Reader first saying

A Reading (Lesson) from ―――――.

A citation giving chapter and verse may be added.

After each Lesson the Reader may say

       The Word of the Lord.
Answer   Thanks be to God.

Or the Reader may say   Here ends the Lesson (Reading).

Silence may be kept after each Reading. One of the following Canticles, or one of those on pages 47-52 (Canticles 1-7), is sung or said after each Reading. If three Lessons are used, the Lesson from the Gospel is read after the second Canticle.

8 The Song of Moses *Cantemus Domino*
Exodus 15:1-6, 11-13, 17-18

Especially suitable for use in Easter Season

I will sing to the Lord, for he is lofty and uplifted; *
  the horse and its rider has he hurled into the sea.
The Lord is my strength and my refuge; *
  the Lord has become my Savior.
This is my God and I will praise him, *
  the God of my people and I will exalt him.
The Lord is a mighty warrior; *
  Yahweh is his Name.
The chariots of Pharaoh and his army has he hurled into the sea; *
  the finest of those who bear armor have been
              drowned in the Red Sea.
The fathomless deep has overwhelmed them; *
  they sank into the depths like a stone.
Your right hand, O Lord, is glorious in might; *
  your right hand, O Lord, has overthrown the enemy.
Who can be compared with you, O Lord, among the gods? *
  who is like you, glorious in holiness,
  awesome in renown, and worker of wonders?
You stretched forth your right hand; *
  the earth swallowed them up.
With your constant love you led the people you redeemed; *
  with your might you brought them in safety to
              your holy dwelling.
You will bring them in and plant them *
  on the mount of your possession,
The resting-place you have made for yourself, O Lord, *
  the sanctuary, O Lord, that your hand has established.
The Lord shall reign *
  for ever and for ever.

Glory to the Father, and to the Son, and to the Holy Spirit: *
  as it was in the beginning, is now, and will be for ever. Amen.

9 The First Song of Isaiah *Ecce, Deus*
Isaiah 12:2-6

Surely, it is God who saves me; *
 I will trust in him and not be afraid.
For the Lord is my stronghold and my sure defense, *
 and he will be my Savior.
Therefore you shall draw water with rejoicing *
 from the springs of salvation.
And on that day you shall say, *
 Give thanks to the Lord and call upon his Name;
Make his deeds known among the peoples; *
 see that they remember that his Name is exalted.
Sing the praises of the Lord, for he has done great things, *
 and this is known in all the world.
Cry aloud, inhabitants of Zion, ring out your joy, *
 for the great one in the midst of you is the Holy One of Israel.

Glory to the Father, and to the Son, and to the Holy Spirit: *
 as it was in the beginning, is now, and will be for ever. Amen

10 The Second Song of Isaiah *Quærite Dominum*
Isaiah 55:6-11

Seek the Lord while he wills to be found; *
 call upon him when he draws near.
Let the wicked forsake their ways *
 and the evil ones their thoughts;
And let them turn to the Lord, and he will have compassion, *
 and to our God, for he will richly pardon.
For my thoughts are not your thoughts, *
 nor your ways my ways, says the Lord.
For as the heavens are higher than the earth, *
 so are my ways higher than your ways,
 and my thoughts than your thoughts.

For as rain and snow fall from the heavens *
    and return not again, but water the earth,
Bringing forth life and giving growth, *
    seed for sowing and bread for eating,
So is my word that goes forth from my mouth; *
    it will not return to me empty;
But it will accomplish that which I have purposed, *
    and prosper in that for which I sent it.

Glory to the Father, and to the Son, and to the Holy Spirit: *
    as it was in the beginning, is now, and will be for ever. Amen.

11   The Third Song of Isaiah   *Surge, illuminare*
Isaiah 60:1-3, 11a, 14c, 18-19

Arise, shine, for your light has come, *
    and the glory of the Lord has dawned upon you.
For behold, darkness covers the land; *
    deep gloom enshrouds the peoples.
But over you the Lord will rise, *
    and his glory will appear upon you.
Nations will stream to your light, *
    and kings to the brightness of your dawning.
Your gates will always be open; *
    by day or night they will never be shut.
They will call you, The City of the Lord, *
    The Zion of the Holy One of Israel.
Violence will no more be heard in your land, *
    ruin or destruction within your borders.
You will call your walls, Salvation, *
    and all your portals, Praise.
The sun will no more be your light by day; *
    by night you will not need the brightness of the moon.

The Lord will be your everlasting light, *
  and your God will be your glory.

Glory to the Father, and to the Son, and to the Holy Spirit: *
  as it was in the beginning, is now, and will be for ever. Ame

12   A Song of Creation   *Benedicite, omnia opera Domini*
Song of the Three Young Men, 35-65

One or more sections of this Canticle may be used. Whatever the selection, it begins with the Invocation and concludes with the Doxology.

Invocation

Glorify the Lord, all you works of the Lord, *
  praise him and highly exalt him for ever.
In the firmament of his power, glorify the Lord, *
  praise him and highly exalt him for ever.

I   The Cosmic Order

Glorify the Lord, you angels and all powers of the Lord, *
  O heavens and all waters above the heavens.
Sun and moon and stars of the sky, glorify the Lord, *
  praise him and highly exalt him for ever.

Glorify the Lord, every shower of rain and fall of dew, *
  all winds and fire and heat.
Winter and summer, glorify the Lord, *
  praise him and highly exalt him for ever.

Glorify the Lord, O chill and cold, *
  drops of dew and flakes of snow.
Frost and cold, ice and sleet, glorify the Lord, *
  praise him and highly exalt him for ever.

Glorify the Lord, O nights and days, *
    O shining light and enfolding dark.
Storm clouds and thunderbolts, glorify the Lord, *
    praise him and highly exalt him for ever.

II   *The Earth and its Creatures*

Let the earth glorify the Lord, *
    praise him and highly exalt him for ever.
Glorify the Lord, O mountains and hills,
and all that grows upon the earth, *
    praise him and highly exalt him for ever.

Glorify the Lord, O springs of water, seas, and streams, *
    O whales and all that move in the waters.
All birds of the air, glorify the Lord, *
    praise him and highly exalt him for ever.

Glorify the Lord, O beasts of the wild, *
    and all you flocks and herds.
O men and women everywhere, glorify the Lord, *
    praise him and highly exalt him for ever.

III   *The People of God*

Let the people of God glorify the Lord, *
    praise him and highly exalt him for ever.
Glorify the Lord, O priests and servants of the Lord, *
    praise him and highly exalt him for ever.

Glorify the Lord, O spirits and souls of the righteous, *
    praise him and highly exalt him for ever.
You that are holy and humble of heart, glorify the Lord, *
    praise him and highly exalt him for ever.

Doxology

Let us glorify the Lord: Father, Son, and Holy Spirit; *
  praise him and highly exalt him for ever.
In the firmament of his power, glorify the Lord, *
  praise him and highly exalt him for ever.

13   A Song of Praise   *Benedictus es, Domine*
Song of the Three Young Men, 29-34

Glory to you, Lord God of our fathers; *
  you are worthy of praise; glory to you.
Glory to you for the radiance of your holy Name; *
  we will praise you and highly exalt you for ever.

Glory to you in the splendor of your temple; *
  on the throne of your majesty, glory to you.
Glory to you, seated between the Cherubim; *
  we will praise you and highly exalt you for ever.

Glory to you, beholding the depths; *
  in the high vault of heaven, glory to you.
Glory to you, Father, Son, and Holy Spirit; *
  we will praise you and highly exalt you for ever.

14   A Song of Penitence   *Kyrie Pantokrator*
Prayer of Manasseh, 1-2, 4, 6-7, 11-15

Especially suitable in Lent, and on other penitential occasions

O Lord and Ruler of the hosts of heaven, *
  God of Abraham, Isaac, and Jacob,
  and of all their righteous offspring:
You made the heavens and the earth, *
  with all their vast array.

All things quake with fear at your presence; *
　　they tremble because of your power.
But your merciful promise is beyond all measure; *
　　it surpasses all that our minds can fathom.
O Lord, you are full of compassion, *
　　long-suffering, and abounding in mercy.
You hold back your hand; *
　　you do not punish as we deserve.
In your great goodness, Lord,
you have promised forgiveness to sinners, *
　　that they may repent of their sin and be saved.
And now, O Lord, I bend the knee of my heart, *
　　and make my appeal, sure of your gracious goodness.
I have sinned, O Lord, I have sinned, *
　　and I know my wickedness only too well.
Therefore I make this prayer to you: *
　　Forgive me, Lord, forgive me.
Do not let me perish in my sin, *
　　nor condemn me to the depths of the earth.
For you, O Lord, are the God of those who repent, *
　　and in me you will show forth your goodness.
Unworthy as I am, you will save me,
in accordance with your great mercy, *
　　and I will praise you without ceasing all the days of my life.
For all the powers of heaven sing your praises, *
　　and yours is the glory to ages of ages. Amen.

15　The Song of Mary　*Magnificat*
Luke 1:46-55

My soul proclaims the greatness of the Lord,
my spirit rejoices in God my Savior; *
　　for he has looked with favor on his lowly servant.

From this day all generations will call me blessed: *
 the Almighty has done great things for me,
 and holy is his Name.
He has mercy on those who fear him *
 in every generation.
He has shown the strength of his arm, *
 he has scattered the proud in their conceit.
He has cast down the mighty from their thrones, *
 and has lifted up the lowly.
He has filled the hungry with good things, *
 and the rich he has sent away empty.
He has come to the help of his servant Israel, *
 for he has remembered his promise of mercy,
The promise he made to our fathers, *
 to Abraham and his children for ever.

Glory to the Father, and to the Son, and to the Holy Spirit: *
 as it was in the beginning, is now, and will be for ever. Amen

16 The Song of Zechariah *Benedictus Dominus Deus*
Luke 1:68-79

Blessed be the Lord, the God of Israel; *
 he has come to his people and set them free.
He has raised up for us a mighty savior, *
 born of the house of his servant David.
Through his holy prophets he promised of old,
 that he would save us from our enemies, *
 from the hands of all who hate us.
He promised to show mercy to our fathers *
 and to remember his holy covenant.
This was the oath he swore to our father Abraham, *
 to set us free from the hands of our enemies,
Free to worship him without fear, *
 holy and righteous in his sight
 all the days of our life.

You, my child, shall be called the prophet of the Most High, *
  for you will go before the Lord to prepare his way,
To give his people knowledge of salvation *
  by the forgiveness of their sins.
In the tender compassion of our God *
  the dawn from on high shall break upon us,
To shine on those who dwell in darkness and the
                  shadow of death, *
  and to guide our feet into the way of peace.

Glory to the Father, and to the Son, and to the Holy Spirit: *
  as it was in the beginning, is now, and will be for ever. Amen.

17   The Song of Simeon   *Nunc dimittis*
   Luke 2:29-32

Lord, you now have set your servant free *
  to go in peace as you have promised;
For these eyes of mine have seen the Savior, *
  whom you have prepared for all the world to see:
A Light to enlighten the nations, *
  and the glory of your people Israel.

Glory to the Father, and to the Son, and to the Holy Spirit: *
  as it was in the beginning, is now, and will be for ever. Amen.

18   A Song to the Lamb   *Dignus es*
   Revelation 4:11; 5:9-10, 13

Splendor and honor and kingly power *
  are yours by right, O Lord our God,
For you created everything that is, *
  and by your will they were created and have their being;

And yours by right, O Lamb that was slain, *
    for with your blood you have redeemed for God,
From every family, language, people, and nation, *
    a kingdom of priests to serve our God.

And so, to him who sits upon the throne, *
    and to Christ the Lamb,
Be worship and praise, dominion and splendor, *
    for ever and for evermore.

19   The Song of the Redeemed   *Magna et mirabilia*
Revelation 15:3-4

O ruler of the universe, Lord God,
great deeds are they that you have done, *
    surpassing human understanding.
Your ways are ways of righteousness and truth, *
    O King of all the ages.

Who can fail to do you homage, Lord,
and sing the praises of your Name? *
    for you only are the holy One.
All nations will draw near and fall down before you, *
    because your just and holy works have been revealed.

Glory to the Father, and to the Son, and to the Holy Spirit: *
    as it was in the beginning, is now, and will be for ever. Amen

20   Glory to God   *Gloria in excelsis*

Glory to God in the highest,
    and peace to his people on earth.

Lord God, heavenly King,
almighty God and Father,

we worship you, we give you thanks,
we praise you for your glory.

Lord Jesus Christ, only Son of the Father,
Lord God, Lamb of God,
you take away the sin of the world;
    have mercy on us;
you are seated at the right hand of the Father;
    receive our prayer.

For you alone are the Holy One,
you alone are the Lord,
you alone are the Most High,
    Jesus Christ,
    with the Holy Spirit,
    in the glory of God the Father. Amen.

21   You are God   *Te Deum laudamus*

You are God: we praise you;
You are the Lord: we acclaim you;
You are the eternal Father:
All creation worships you.
To you all angels, all the powers of heaven,
Cherubim and Seraphim, sing in endless praise:
    Holy, holy, holy Lord, God of power and might,
    heaven and earth are full of your glory.
The glorious company of apostles praise you.
The noble fellowship of prophets praise you.
The white-robed army of martyrs praise you.
Throughout the world the holy Church acclaims you;
    Father, of majesty unbounded,
    your true and only Son, worthy of all worship,
    and the Holy Spirit, advocate and guide.

You, Christ, are the king of glory,
the eternal Son of the Father.
When you became man to set us free
you did not shun the Virgin's womb.
You overcame the sting of death
and opened the kingdom of heaven to all believers.
You are seated at God's right hand in glory.
We believe that you will come and be our judge.
> Come then, Lord, and help your people,
> bought with the price of your own blood,
> and bring us with your saints
> to glory everlasting.

The Apostles' Creed

Officiant and People together, all standing

I believe in God, the Father almighty,
> creator of heaven and earth.
I believe in Jesus Christ, his only Son, our Lord.
> He was conceived by the power of the Holy Spirit
> > and born of the Virgin Mary.
> He suffered under Pontius Pilate,
> > was crucified, died, and was buried.
> He descended to the dead.
> On the third day he rose again.
> He ascended into heaven,
> > and is seated at the right hand of the Father.
> He will come again to judge the living and the dead.
I believe in the Holy Spirit,
> the holy catholic Church,
> the communion of saints,
> the forgiveness of sins,
> the resurrection of the body,
> and the life everlasting. Amen.

The Prayers

The people stand or kneel

Officiant	The Lord be with you.
People	And also with you.
Officiant	Let us pray.

Officiant and People

Our Father, who art in heaven,
    hallowed be thy Name,
    thy kingdom come,
    thy will be done,
        on earth as it is in heaven.
Give us this day our daily bread.
And forgive us our trespasses,
    as we forgive those
        who trespass against us.
And lead us not into temptation,
    but deliver us from evil.
For thine is the kingdom,
    and the power, and the glory,
    for ever and ever. Amen.
	Our Father in heaven,
	    hallowed be your Name,
	    your kingdom come,
	    your will be done,
	        on earth as in heaven.
	Give us today our daily bread.
	Forgive us our sins
	    as we forgive those
	        who sin against us.
	Save us from the time of trial,
	    and deliver us from evil.
	For the kingdom, the power,
	    and the glory are yours,
	    now and for ever. Amen.

Then follows one of these sets of Suffrages

A

V.	Show us your mercy, O Lord;
R.	And grant us your salvation.
V.	Clothe your ministers with righteousness;
R.	Let your people sing with joy.
V.	Give peace, O Lord, in all the world;
R.	For only in you can we live in safety.

V. Lord, keep this nation under your care;
R. And guide us in the way of justice and truth.
V. Let your way be known upon earth;
R. Your saving health among all nations.
V. Let not the needy, O Lord, be forgotten;
R. Nor the hope of the poor be taken away.
V. Create in us clean hearts, O God;
R. And sustain us with your Holy Spirit.

B

V. Save your people, Lord, and bless your inheritance;
R. Govern and uphold them, now and always.
V. Day by day we bless you;
R. We praise your Name for ever.
V. Lord, keep us from all sin today;
R. Have mercy on us, Lord, have mercy.
V. Lord, show us your love and mercy;
R. For we put our trust in you.
V. In you, Lord, is our hope;
R. And we shall never hope in vain.

The Officiant then says one or more of the following Collects

The Collect of the Day

A Collect for Sundays

O God, you make us glad with the weekly remembrance of the glorious resurrection of your Son our Lord: Give us this day such blessing through our worship of you, that the week to come may be spent in your favor; through Jesus Christ our Lord. *Amen.*

A Collect for Fridays

Almighty God, whose most dear Son went not up to joy but first he suffered pain, and entered not into glory before he was crucified: Mercifully grant that we, walking in the way of the cross, may find it none other than the way of life and peace; through Jesus Christ your Son our Lord. *Amen.*

A Collect for Saturdays

Almighty God, who after the creation of the world rested from all your works and sanctified a day of rest for all your creatures: Grant that we, putting away all earthly anxieties, may be duly prepared for the service of your sanctuary, and that our rest here upon earth may be a preparation for the eternal rest promised to your people in heaven; through Jesus Christ our Lord. *Amen.*

A Collect for the Renewal of Life

O God, the King eternal, whose light divides the day from the night and turns the shadow of death into the morning: Drive far from us all wrong desires, incline our hearts to keep your law, and guide our feet into the way of peace; that, having done your will with cheerfulness during the day, we may, when night comes, rejoice to give you thanks; through Jesus Christ our Lord. *Amen.*

A Collect for Peace

O God, the author of peace and lover of concord, to know you is eternal life and to serve you is perfect freedom: Defend us, your humble servants, in all assaults of our enemies; that we, surely trusting in your defense, may not fear the power of any adversaries; through the might of Jesus Christ our Lord. *Amen.*

A Collect for Grace

Lord God, almighty and everlasting Father, you have brought us in safety to this new day: Preserve us with your mighty power, that we may not fall into sin, nor be overcome by adversity; and in all we do, direct us to the fulfilling of your purpose; through Jesus Christ our Lord. *Amen.*

A Collect for Guidance

Heavenly Father, in you we live and move and have our being: We humbly pray you so to guide and govern us by your Holy Spirit, that in all the cares and occupations of our life we may not forget you, but may remember that we are ever walking in your sight; through Jesus Christ our Lord. *Amen.*

Then, unless the Eucharist or a form of general intercession is to follow, one of these prayers for mission is added

Almighty and everlasting God, by whose Spirit the whole body of your faithful people is governed and sanctified: Receive our supplications and prayers which we offer before you for all members of your holy Church, that in their vocation and ministry they may truly and devoutly serve you; through our Lord and Savior Jesus Christ. *Amen.*

or this

O God, you have made of one blood all the peoples of the earth, and sent your blessed Son to preach peace to those who are far off and to those who are near: Grant that people everywhere may seek after you and find you; bring the nations into your fold; pour out your Spirit upon all flesh; and hasten the coming of your kingdom; through Jesus Christ our Lord. *Amen.*

or the following

Lord Jesus Christ, you stretched out your arms of love on the hard wood of the cross that everyone might come within the reach of your saving embrace: So clothe us in your Spirit that we, reaching forth our hands in love, may bring those who do not know you to the knowledge and love of you; for the honor of your Name. *Amen.*

Here may be sung a hymn or anthem.

Authorized intercessions and thanksgivings may follow.

Before the close of the Office one or both of the following may be used

The General Thanksgiving

Officiant and People

Almighty God, Father of all mercies,
we your unworthy servants give you humble thanks
for all your goodness and loving-kindness
to us and to all whom you have made.
We bless you for our creation, preservation,
and all the blessings of this life;
but above all for your immeasurable love
in the redemption of the world by our Lord Jesus Christ;
for the means of grace, and for the hope of glory.
And, we pray, give us such an awareness of your mercies,
that with truly thankful hearts we may show forth your praise,
not only with our lips, but in our lives,
by giving up our selves to your service,
and by walking before you
in holiness and righteousness all our days;
through Jesus Christ our Lord,
to whom, with you and the Holy Spirit,
be honor and glory throughout all ages. Amen.

A Prayer of St. Chrysostom

Almighty God, you have given us grace at this time with one accord to make our common supplication to you; and you have promised through your well-beloved Son that when two or three are gathered together in his Name you will be in the midst of them: Fulfill now, O Lord, our desires and petitions as may be best for us; granting us in this world knowledge of your truth, and in the age to come life everlasting. *Amen.*

Then may be said

Let us bless the Lord.
Thanks be to God.

From Easter Day through the Day of Pentecost "Alleluia, alleluia" may be added to the preceding versicle and response.

The Officiant may then conclude with one of the following

The grace of our Lord Jesus Christ, and the love of God, and the fellowship of the Holy Spirit, be with us all evermore. *Amen.*   *2 Corinthians 13:14*

May the God of hope fill us with all joy and peace in believing through the power of the Holy Spirit. *Amen.*
Romans 15:13

Glory to God whose power, working in us, can do infinitely more than we can ask or imagine: Glory to him from generation to generation in the Church, and in Christ Jesus for ever and ever. *Amen.*   *Ephesians 3:20, 21*

An Order of Service for Noonday

Officiant   O God, make speed to save us.
People   O Lord, make haste to help us.

Officiant and People

Glory to the Father, and to the Son, and to the Holy Spirit: as it was in the beginning, is now, and will be for ever. Amen.

Except in Lent, add   Alleluia.

A suitable hymn may be sung.

One or more of the following Psalms is sung or said. Other suitable selections include Psalms 19, 67, one or more sections of Psalm 119, or a selection from Psalms 120 through 133.

Psalm 119   *Lucerna pedibus meis*

105   Your word is a lantern to my feet *
    and a light upon my path.

106   I have sworn and am determined *
    to keep your righteous judgments.

107 I am deeply troubled; *
 preserve my life, O Lord, according to your word.

108 Accept, O Lord, the willing tribute of my lips, *
 and teach me your judgments.

109 My life is always in my hand, *
 yet I do not forget your law.

110 The wicked have set a trap for me, *
 but I have not strayed from your commandments.

111 Your decrees are my inheritance for ever; *
 truly, they are the joy of my heart.

112 I have applied my heart to fulfill your statutes *
 for ever and to the end.

Psalm 121 *Levavi oculos*

1 I lift up my eyes to the hills; *
 from where is my help to come?

2 My help comes from the Lord, *
 the maker of heaven and earth.

3 He will not let your foot be moved *
 and he who watches over you will not fall asleep.

4 Behold, he who keeps watch over Israel *
 shall neither slumber nor sleep;

5 The Lord himself watches over you; *
 the Lord is your shade at your right hand,

6 So that the sun shall not strike you by day, *
 nor the moon by night.

7 The Lord shall preserve you from all evil; *
 it is he who shall keep you safe.

8 The Lord shall watch over your going out and
            your coming in, *
    from this time forth for evermore.

Psalm 126 *In convertendo*

1 When the Lord restored the fortunes of Zion, *
    then were we like those who dream.

2 Then was our mouth filled with laughter, *
    and our tongue with shouts of joy.

3 Then they said among the nations, *
    "The Lord has done great things for them."

4 The Lord has done great things for us, *
    and we are glad indeed.

5 Restore our fortunes, O Lord, *
    like the watercourses of the Negev.

6 Those who sowed with tears *
    will reap with songs of joy.

7 Those who go out weeping, carrying the seed, *
    will come again with joy, shouldering their sheaves.

At the end of the Psalms is sung or said

Glory to the Father, and to the Son, and to the Holy Spirit: *
as it was in the beginning, is now, and will be for ever. Amen.

One of the following, or some other suitable passage of Scripture, is read

The love of God has been poured into our hearts through the Holy Spirit that has been given to us.   *Romans 5:5*

People   Thanks be to God.

or the following

If anyone is in Christ he is a new creation; the old has passed away, behold the new has come. All this is from God, who through Christ reconciled us to himself and gave us the ministry of reconciliation.   *2 Corinthians 5:17-18*

People   Thanks be to God.

or this

From the rising of the sun to its setting my Name shall be great among the nations, and in every place incense shall be offered to my Name, and a pure offering; for my Name shall be great among the nations, says the Lord of Hosts.   *Malachi 1:11*

People   Thanks be to God.

A meditation, silent or spoken, may follow.

The Officiant then begins the Prayers

Lord, have mercy.
Christ, have mercy.
Lord, have mercy.

Officiant and People

Our Father, who art in heaven,
    hallowed be thy Name,
    thy kingdom come,
    thy will be done,
        on earth as it is in heaven.
Give us this day our daily bread.
And forgive us our trespasses,
    as we forgive those
        who trespass against us.
And lead us not into temptation,
    but deliver us from evil.
	Our Father in heaven,
	    hallowed be your Name,
	    your kingdom come,
	    your will be done,
	        on earth as in heaven.
	Give us today our daily bread.
	Forgive us our sins
	    as we forgive those
	        who sin against us.
	Save us from the time of trial,
	    and deliver us from evil.

Officiant Lord, hear our prayer;
People And let our cry come to you.
Officiant Let us pray.

The Officiant then says one of the following Collects. If desired, the Collect of the Day may be used.

Heavenly Father, send your Holy Spirit into our hearts, to direct and rule us according to your will, to comfort us in all our afflictions, to defend us from all error, and to lead us into all truth; through Jesus Christ our Lord. *Amen.*

Blessed Savior, at this hour you hung upon the cross, stretching out your loving arms: Grant that all the peoples of the earth may look to you and be saved; for your tender mercies' sake. *Amen.*

Almighty Savior, who at noonday called your servant Saint Paul to be an apostle to the Gentiles: We pray you to illumine the world with the radiance of your glory, that all nations may come and worship you; for you live and reign for ever and ever. *Amen.*

Lord Jesus Christ, you said to your apostles, "Peace I give to you; my own peace I leave with you:" Regard not our sins, but the faith of your Church, and give to us the peace and unity of that heavenly City, where with the Father and the Holy Spirit you live and reign, now and for ever. *Amen.*

Free intercessions may be offered.

The service concludes as follows

Officiant Let us bless the Lord.
People Thanks be to God.

Daily Evening Prayer: Rite Two

The Officiant begins the service with one or more of the following sentences of Scripture, or of those on pages 75-78;

or with the Service of Light on pages 109-112, and continuing with the appointed Psalmody;

or with the versicle "O God, make speed to save us" on page 117

Let my prayer be set forth in your sight as incense, the lifting up of my hands as the evening sacrifice. *Psalm 141:2*

Grace to you and peace from God our Father and from the Lord Jesus Christ. *Philippians 1:2*

Worship the Lord in the beauty of holiness; let the whole earth tremble before him. *Psalm 96:9*

Yours is the day, O God, yours also the night; you established the moon and the sun. You fixed all the boundaries of the earth; you made both summer and winter. *Psalm 74:15,16*

I will bless the Lord who gives me counsel; my heart teaches me, night after night. I have set the Lord always before me; because he is at my right hand, I shall not fall. *Psalm 16:7,8*

Seek him who made the Pleiades and Orion, and turns deep darkness into the morning, and darkens the day into night; who calls for the waters of the sea and pours them out upon the surface of the earth: The Lord is his name. *Amos 5:8*

If I say, "Surely the darkness will cover me, and the light around me turn to night," darkness is not dark to you, O Lord; the night is as bright as the day; darkness and light to you are both alike.   *Psalm 139:10, 11*

Jesus said, "I am the light of the world; whoever follows me will not walk in darkness, but will have the light of life." *John 8:12*

The following Confession of Sin may then be said; or the Office may continue at once with "O God make speed to save us."

Confession of Sin

The Officiant says to the people

Dear friends in Christ, here in the presence of Almighty God, let us kneel in silence, and with penitent and obedient hearts confess our sins, so that we may obtain forgiveness by his infinite goodness and mercy.

or this

Let us confess our sins against God and our neighbor.

Silence may be kept.

Officiant and People together, all kneeling

Most merciful God,
we confess that we have sinned against you
in thought, word, and deed,
by what we have done,
and by what we have left undone.
We have not loved you with our whole heart;
we have not loved our neighbors as ourselves.
We are truly sorry and we humbly repent.

For the sake of your Son Jesus Christ,
have mercy on us and forgive us;
that we may delight in your will,
and walk in your ways,
to the glory of your Name. Amen.

The Priest alone stands and says

Almighty God have mercy on you, forgive you all your
sins through our Lord Jesus Christ, strengthen you in all
goodness, and by the power of the Holy Spirit keep you in
eternal life. *Amen.*

*A deacon or lay person using the preceding form remains kneeling, and
substitutes "us" for "you" and "our" for "your."*

The Invitatory and Psalter

All stand

Officiant	O God, make speed to save us.
People	O Lord, make haste to help us.

Officiant and People

Glory to the Father, and to the Son, and to the Holy Spirit: as
it was in the beginning, is now, and will be for ever. Amen.

Except in Lent, add Alleluia.

*The following, or some other suitable hymn, or an Invitatory Psalm, may
be sung or said*

O Gracious Light *Phos hilaron*

O gracious Light,
pure brightness of the everliving Father in heaven,
O Jesus Christ, holy and blessed!

Now as we come to the setting of the sun,
and our eyes behold the vesper light,
we sing your praises, O God: Father, Son, and Holy Spirit.

You are worthy at all times to be praised by happy voices,
O Son of God, O Giver of life,
and to be glorified through all the worlds.

Then follows

The Psalm or Psalms Appointed

At the end of the Psalms is sung or said

Glory to the Father, and to the Son, and to the Holy Spirit: *
as it was in the beginning, is now, and will be for ever. Amen.

The Lessons

One or two Lessons, as appointed, are read, the Reader first saying

A Reading (Lesson) from _____ .

A citation giving chapter and verse may be added.

After each Lesson the Reader may say

        The Word of the Lord.
Answer   Thanks be to God.

Or the Reader may say   Here ends the Lesson (Reading).

Silence may be kept after each Reading. One of the following Canticles, or one of those on pages 47-52, or 85-95, is sung or said after each Reading. If three Lessons are used, the Lesson from the Gospel is read after the second Canticle.

The Song of Mary   *Magnificat*

Luke 1:46-55

My soul proclaims the greatness of the Lord,
my spirit rejoices in God my Savior; *
    for he has looked with favor on his lowly servant.
From this day all generations will call me blessed: *
    the Almighty has done great things for me,
    and holy is his Name.
He has mercy on those who fear him *
    in every generation.
He has shown the strength of his arm, *
    he has scattered the proud in their conceit.
He has cast down the mighty from their thrones, *
    and has lifted up the lowly.
He has filled the hungry with good things, *
    and the rich he has sent away empty.
He has come to the help of his servant Israel, *
    for he has remembered his promise of mercy,
The promise he made to our fathers, *
    to Abraham and his children for ever.

Glory to the Father, and to the Son, and to the Holy Spirit: *
    as it was in the beginning, is now, and will be for ever. Amen.

The Song of Simeon   *Nunc dimittis*

Luke 2:29-32

Lord, you now have set your servant free *
　to go in peace as you have promised;
For these eyes of mine have seen the Savior, *
　whom you have prepared for all the world to see:
A Light to enlighten the nations, *
　and the glory of your people Israel.

Glory to the Father, and to the Son, and to the Holy Spirit: *
　as it was in the beginning, is now, and will be for ever. Amen

The Apostles' Creed

Officiant and People together, all standing

I believe in God, the Father almighty,
　creator of heaven and earth.
I believe in Jesus Christ, his only Son, our Lord.
　　He was conceived by the power of the Holy Spirit
　　　and born of the Virgin Mary.
　　He suffered under Pontius Pilate,
　　　was crucified, died, and was buried.
　　He descended to the dead.
　　On the third day he rose again.
　　He ascended into heaven,
　　　and is seated at the right hand of the Father.
　　He will come again to judge the living and the dead.
I believe in the Holy Spirit,
　the holy catholic Church,
　the communion of saints,
　the forgiveness of sins,
　the resurrection of the body,
　and the life everlasting. Amen.

The Prayers

The people stand or kneel

Officiant The Lord be with you.
People   And also with you.
Officiant Let us pray.

Officiant and People

Our Father, who art in heaven,
    hallowed be thy Name,
    thy kingdom come,
    thy will be done,
        on earth as it is in heaven.
Give us this day our daily bread.
And forgive us our trespasses,
    as we forgive those
        who trespass against us.
And lead us not into temptation,
    but deliver us from evil.
For thine is the kingdom,
    and the power, and the glory,
    for ever and ever. Amen.
	Our Father in heaven,
	    hallowed be your Name,
	    your kingdom come,
	    your will be done,
	        on earth as in heaven.
	Give us today our daily bread.
	Forgive us our sins
	    as we forgive those
	        who sin against us.
	Save us from the time of trial,
	    and deliver us from evil.
	For the kingdom, the power,
	    and the glory are yours,
	    now and for ever. Amen.

Then follows one of these sets of Suffrages

A

V. Show us your mercy, O Lord;
R. And grant us your salvation.
V. Clothe your ministers with righteousness;
R. Let your people sing with joy.
V. Give peace, O Lord, in all the world;
R. For only in you can we live in safety.

V. Lord, keep this nation under your care;
R. And guide us in the way of justice and truth.
V. Let your way be known upon earth;
R. Your saving health among all nations.
V. Let not the needy, O Lord, be forgotten;
R. Nor the hope of the poor be taken away.
V. Create in us clean hearts, O God;
R. And sustain us with your Holy Spirit.

B

That this evening may be holy, good, and peaceful,
We entreat you, O Lord.

That your holy angels may lead us in paths of peace and goodwill,
We entreat you, O Lord.

That we may be pardoned and forgiven for our sins and offenses,
We entreat you, O Lord.

That there may be peace to your Church and to the whole world,
We entreat you, O Lord.

That we may depart this life in your faith and fear, and not be condemned before the great judgment seat of Christ,
We entreat you, O Lord.

That we may be bound together by your Holy Spirit in the communion of [_____ and] all your saints, entrusting one another and all our life to Christ,
We entreat you, O Lord.

The Officiant then says one or more of the following Collects

The Collect of the Day

A *Collect for Sundays*

Lord God, whose Son our Savior Jesus Christ triumphed over the powers of death and prepared for us our place in the new Jerusalem: Grant that we, who have this day given thanks for his resurrection, may praise you in that City of which he is the light, and where he lives and reigns for ever and ever. *Amen.*

A *Collect for Fridays*

Lord Jesus Christ, by your death you took away the sting of death: Grant to us your servants so to follow in faith where you have led the way, that we may at length fall asleep peacefully in you and wake up in your likeness; for your tender mercies' sake. *Amen.*

A *Collect for Saturdays*

O God, the source of eternal light: Shed forth your unending day upon us who watch for you, that our lips may praise you, our lives may bless you, and our worship on the morrow give you glory; through Jesus Christ our Lord. *Amen.*

A *Collect for Peace*

Most holy God, the source of all good desires, all right judgments, and all just works: Give to us, your servants, that peace which the world cannot give, so that our minds may be fixed on the doing of your will, and that we, being delivered from the fear of all enemies, may live in peace and quietness; through the mercies of Christ Jesus our Savior. *Amen.*

A *Collect for Aid against Perils*

Be our light in the darkness, O Lord, and in your great mercy defend us from all perils and dangers of this night; for the love of your only Son, our Savior Jesus Christ. *Amen.*

A Collect for Protection

O God, the life of all who live, the light of the faithful, the strength of those who labor, and the repose of the dead: We thank you for the blessings of the day that is past, and humbly ask for your protection through the coming night. Bring us in safety to the morning hours; through him who died and rose again for us, your Son our Savior Jesus Christ. *Amen.*

A Collect for the Presence of Christ

Lord Jesus, stay with us, for evening is at hand and the day is past; be our companion in the way, kindle our hearts, and awaken hope, that we may know you as you are revealed in Scripture and the breaking of bread. Grant this for the sake of your love. *Amen.*

Then, unless the Eucharist or a form of general intercession is to follow, one of these prayers for mission is added

O God and Father of all, whom the whole heavens adore: Let the whole earth also worship you, all nations obey you, all tongues confess and bless you, and men and women everywhere love you and serve you in peace; through Jesus Christ our Lord. *Amen.*

or this

Keep watch, dear Lord, with those who work, or watch, or weep this night, and give your angels charge over those who sleep. Tend the sick, Lord Christ; give rest to the weary, bless the dying, soothe the suffering, pity the afflicted, shield the joyous; and all for your love's sake. *Amen.*

or the following

O God, you manifest in your servants the signs of your presence: Send forth upon us the Spirit of love, that in companionship with one another your abounding grace may increase among us; through Jesus Christ our Lord. *Amen.*

Here may be sung a hymn or anthem.

Authorized intercessions and thanksgivings may follow.

Before the close of the Office one or both of the following may be used

The General Thanksgiving

Officiant and People

Almighty God, Father of all mercies,
we your unworthy servants give you humble thanks
for all your goodness and loving-kindness
to us and to all whom you have made.
We bless you for our creation, preservation,
and all the blessings of this life;
but above all for your immeasurable love
in the redemption of the world by our Lord Jesus Christ;
for the means of grace, and for the hope of glory.
And, we pray, give us such an awareness of your mercies,
that with truly thankful hearts we may show forth your praise,
not only with our lips, but in our lives,
by giving up our selves to your service,
and by walking before you
in holiness and righteousness all our days;
through Jesus Christ our Lord,
to whom, with you and the Holy Spirit,
be honor and glory throughout all ages. Amen.

A Prayer of St. Chrysostom

Almighty God, you have given us grace at this time with one accord to make our common supplication to you; and you have promised through your well-beloved Son that when two or three are gathered together in his Name you will be in the midst of them: Fulfill now, O Lord, our desires and petitions as may be best for us; granting us in this world knowledge of your truth, and in the age to come life everlasting. *Amen.*

Then may be said

Let us bless the Lord.
Thanks be to God.

From Easter Day through the Day of Pentecost "Alleluia, alleluia" may be added to the preceding versicle and response.

The Officiant may then conclude with one of the following

The grace of our Lord Jesus Christ, and the love of God, and the fellowship of the Holy Spirit, be with us all evermore. *Amen.*   2 *Corinthians 13:14*

May the God of hope fill us with all joy and peace in believing through the power of the Holy Spirit. *Amen.*
Romans 15:13

Glory to God whose power, working in us, can do infinitely more than we can ask or imagine: Glory to him from generation to generation in the Church, and in Christ Jesus for ever and ever. *Amen.*   *Ephesians 3:20,21*

Daily Devotions for Individuals and Families

These devotions follow the basic structure of the Daily Office of the Church.

When more than one person is present, the Reading and the Collect should be read by one person, and the other parts said in unison, or in some other convenient manner. (For suggestions about reading the Psalms, see page 582.)

For convenience, appropriate Psalms, Readings, and Collects are provided in each service. When desired, however, the Collect of the Day, or any of the Collects appointed in the Daily Offices, may be used instead.

The Psalms and Readings may be replaced by those appointed in

a) the Lectionary for Sundays, Holy Days, the Common of Saints, and Various Occasions, page 888

b) the Daily Office Lectionary, page 934

c) some other manual of devotion which provides daily selections for the Church Year.

In the Morning

From Psalm 51

Open my lips, O Lord, *
 and my mouth shall proclaim your praise.
Create in me a clean heart, O God, *
 and renew a right spirit within me.
Cast me not away from your presence *
 and take not your holy Spirit from me.
Give me the joy of your saving help again *
 and sustain me with your bountiful Spirit.
Glory to the Father, and to the Son, and to the Holy Spirit: *
 as it was in the beginning, is now, and will be for ever. Amen.

A Reading

Blessed be the God and Father of our Lord Jesus Christ!
By his great mercy we have been born anew to a living hope
through the resurrection of Jesus Christ from the dead.
1 Peter 1:3

A period of silence may follow.

A hymn or canticle may be used; the Apostles' Creed may be said.

Prayers may be offered for ourselves and others.

The Lord's Prayer

The Collect

Lord God, almighty and everlasting Father, you have brought us in safety to this new day: Preserve us with your mighty power, that we may not fall into sin, nor be overcome by adversity; and in all we do, direct us to the fulfilling of your purpose; through Jesus Christ our Lord. *Amen.*

At Noon

From Psalm 113

Give praise, you servants of the Lord; *
　praise the Name of the Lord.
Let the Name of the Lord be blessed, *
　from this time forth for evermore.
From the rising of the sun to its going down *
　let the Name of the Lord be praised.
The Lord is high above all nations, *
　and his glory above the heavens.

A Reading

O God, you will keep in perfect peace those whose minds are fixed on you; for in returning and rest we shall be saved; in quietness and trust shall be our strength.　*Isaiah 26:3; 30:15*

Prayers may be offered for ourselves and others.

The Lord's Prayer

The Collect

Blessed Savior, at this hour you hung upon the cross, stretching out your loving arms: Grant that all the peoples of the earth may look to you and be saved; for your mercies' sake. *Amen.*

or this

Lord Jesus Christ, you said to your apostles, "Peace I give to you; my own peace I leave with you:" Regard not our sins, but the faith of your Church, and give to us the peace and unity of that heavenly City, where with the Father and the Holy Spirit you live and reign, now and for ever. *Amen.*

In the Early Evening

This devotion may be used before or after the evening meal.

The Order of Worship for the Evening, page 109, may be used instead.

O gracious Light,
pure brightness of the everliving Father in heaven,
O Jesus Christ, holy and blessed!

Now as we come to the setting of the sun,
and our eyes behold the vesper light,
we sing your praises O God: Father, Son, and Holy Spirit.

You are worthy at all times to be praised by happy voices,
O Son of God, O Giver of life,
and to be glorified through all the worlds.

A Reading

It is not ourselves that we proclaim; we proclaim Christ Jesus as Lord, and ourselves as your servants, for Jesus' sake. For the same God who said, "Out of darkness let light shine," has caused his light to shine within us, to give the light of revelation—the revelation of the glory of God in the face of Jesus Christ.   *2 Corinthians 4:5-6*

Prayers may be offered for ourselves and others.

The Lord's Prayer

The Collect

Lord Jesus, stay with us, for evening is at hand and the day is past; be our companion in the way, kindle our hearts, and awaken hope, that we may know you as you are revealed in Scripture and the breaking of bread. Grant this for the sake of your love. *Amen.*

At the Close of Day

Psalm 134

Behold now, bless the Lord, all you servants of the Lord, *
   you that stand by night in the house of the Lord.
Lift up your hands in the holy place and bless the Lord; *
   the Lord who made heaven and earth bless you out of Zion.

A Reading

Lord, you are in the midst of us and we are called by your Name: Do not forsake us, O Lord our God.   *Jeremiah 14:9,22*

The following may be said

Lord, you now have set your servant free *
   to go in peace as you have promised;
For these eyes of mine have seen the Savior, *
   whom you have prepared for all the world to see:
A Light to enlighten the nations, *
   and the glory of your people Israel.

Prayers for ourselves and others may follow. It is appropriate that prayers of thanksgiving for the blessings of the day, and penitence for our sins, be included.

The Lord's Prayer

The Collect

Visit this place, O Lord, and drive far from it all snares of the enemy; let your holy angels dwell with us to preserve us in peace; and let your blessing be upon us always; through Jesus Christ our Lord. *Amen.*

The almighty and merciful Lord, Father, Son, and Holy Spirit, bless us and keep us. *Amen.*